HAPPY WEIGHT LOSS

By Irina Ahnland

Published by WriterMotive
www.writermotive.co.uk

Contents

Foreword

This book is a masterpiece that offers a profound insight into how to live a life we earnestly desire and if the instructions are followed religiously, it will produce a shocking result you will be proud of. I am privileged to be one of the editors of this book and it has made a tremendous impact in my life and I believe it will create the same immense impact in your life which you cannot forget in a hurry. The simplicity of its language and vivid illustrations make it relevant to all audiences of different ages, shape and sex.

Irina's painstaking effort in ensuring that this book is well researched is very obvious from the content coupled with her vast experience as a weight loss coach. This book will give you impetus to see all the positive qualities and potentials that are resident inside of you and teach you how you can tap into these potentials and appreciate yourself better than you have ever imagined.

I highly recommend you get a copy for your library and some for your friends and colleagues who are worried about losing weight or love to live a healthy lifestyle.

Akinola Oriola (Ph.D)
English and Literary Studies.

Dedicated to my parents, Lydia and Alexander
for their love, support and belief in me.

Acknowledgement.

I am a lucky person and on my journey I met wonderful and talented people.

I would like to express my profound gratitude to my talented translator, Oxana Chuksina for her professionalism, efficiency, hard work and enthusiasm and my editor, Akinola Oriola for his brilliant and enjoyable cooperation.

Last but not least are my clients, friends and admirers who were a source of encouragement to me during the writing of this book.

Introduction

Overweight and obesity are scourges in our age. Fashion magazines and media praise slenderness and thinness. Millions of people, both male and female, torture themselves with diets, weight loss pills and fitness activities, but every year, the problem of unwanted weight is becoming more actual.

Fashionable diets deplete ration and weaken the immune system, exhausting exercises leads to fatigue and micro trauma, drugs interfere with the natural metabolism and interrupt the operation of the internal organs. The result is undermined health, depression and extra kilos that come back again and again.

It often happens that people drop weight with unbelievable effort and reach their weight loss goal, which they have been dreaming for a long time, but still they don't feel really happy. People admit that nothing has changed in their life except their clothes size. This same lack of confidence and decisiveness, gloom, depression and loss of interest in life persist.

The most important thing people should realise when they wish to lose weight is to stop fighting first, because with the battle you will never create beauty and harmony. Beauty is born in the acceptance and love of yourself and your life. This is the secret of successful weight loss.

This book will provide you with a clear-cut path and it will make your weight loss journey to a New You exciting and pleasant.

I wish you enjoyable reading. Happy Weight Loss!

I. What makes stubborn fat so stubborn.

Chapter 1. Why diets never work and why we fail in losing weight.

Diets have come into our lives so firmly that they have become a way of life and even part of a lifestyle for many people. Every year new books are published with the new miracle diets and detailed instructions about how to make this miracle possible. So a new battle begins with a new zeal, but it leads to another failure and the winner is the unwanted weight in this unequal battle. Who is the loser? It is our body, worn out and exhausted, and sometimes with broken health.

Achieving no result after one diet, many people get on another "more efficient" diet being advertised and this process can continue forever. But the result is always the same - gaining extra kilos and body exhaustion. Some desperate diets followers drive themselves to real mental breakdown.

Why are the diets useless and even dangerous in most cases?

In fact, any diet is stressful to our body. First of all, it's not fat that is burnt, but it is protein that is consumed - the body uses its protein reserves by eating itself. The skin becomes flabby and facial wrinkles appear. Without sufficient protein, the activity of the endocrine glands is disturbed, hormonal changes take place, enzymes production as well as the absorption of important nutrients is disrupted, the production of antibodies is reduced, and thus general immunity weakened. All this is due to the fact that proteins are involved in almost all processes in the body. And without realizing it, you are in a state of war with your own body, causing unrecoverable damage to it and simply depriving yourself of good health.

After a diet, the body begins to fill up the vitamins and minerals deficit and actively gains more fat to reserve it in case of a new battle. As a result, your pre-diet weight not only returns but even increases. Please remember, if you like to lose weight do not go on a diet, do not get trapped anymore.

Why other attempts to lose weight don't bring long lasting results?

After years of experience, I came to the conclusion that there are four major mistakes that people make when they want to lose weight but cannot reach that goal. If you correct these mistakes, you'll succeed, believe me.

The first mistake is uncertainty. This means your goal is not clearly stated or formulated. For example, you say to yourself: "I'll try to get slim, it may probably help me." This is wrong. You must be firm and say "Yes, I want to be slim," "I'll do it!" not "I'll try." Be assertive to achieve your result. Decide how many kilos you want to lose and in what time-period. Enjoy even small changes and positive results because this way you will strengthen your faith in yourself and programme yourself for success.

Your friends' support will help you to cope with uncertainty. Explain the importance of the situation to your family and friends. Ask them to support you on the path to getting fit and they will reciprocate your request by all means. Success cannot be achieved when you are alone on the journey and we can never achieve our goals without the help of others. So feel free about this request and maybe one day you'll be strong enough to support to them.

The second mistake which everyone makes is the desire to get everything at once by all means. Perfectionism is mistakenly believed to be good, but in reality it is perfectionism that often destroys a person's chances to succeed. A person wants to do everything perfectly, but he condemns himself to frustration and a sense of defeat. This in turn reduces every chance for his dream to come true.

Do not be a perfectionist and have patience. It is also easy to handle – you should love not only the result that you want, but the process as well. For example, you've recently started doing morning exercises, which you've never done before or instead of fatty meat, you eat chicken breast or fish with vegetables, which you could hardly have imagined before. You also notice that every day, you feel better and your body becomes more beautiful and stronger, so this is the joy, this is the pleasure of processing your dream and the result won't take you long to see.

Another mistake many people make is the fear of change. People in general do not like changes. They tend to protect their security, their own world that they have created, because it is their own familiar world and it is predictable. It may be a world with not much joy or no interesting events, but still it is their own predictable and safe world.

After all, in order to lose weight, you need to go through changes - change your mindset, your habits and your daily living. Most people think, "What If I cannot manage it? What if I make it only worse? What if I attract more attention of other people to myself and I will not be able to cope with it? Or maybe I'll lose all the good things that I have now in my life - my friends, my routine or something even more personal?".

Is it really worth it to be afraid of changes? Changes are like a fresh breeze, which will fill your life with new dreams, ideas and power. Open the door to a new life and don't look back. You will find so many interesting, wonderful and exciting things waiting for you. Do not betray your happiness through an unhealthy lifestyle, depression and extra weight. Be faithful to your dreams and you will manage!

The fourth common mistake is the fear of many constraints and constant supervision. Yes, of course, some restrictions will take place and you need to have discipline. So enjoy this process and be pleased to realise that you control your life, you achieve your goals and every new day takes you closer to your dreams!

Chapter 2. Let's get started.

Strong motivation is the first step on your journey to your perfect shape. Losing weight will never be achieved if the person does not have clear and specific reasons for it. Moreover, if the motivation is weak, the person will just never take any specific actions to get the result.

Each person is unique and, therefore, the motivation in weight loss must be unique to each individual. The main reason for the failure in losing weight is the fact that many people do not know the honest answer to the main question: "Why do I want to lose weight? "

'In fact, this question is not as simple as it seems, you really have to think it over. If you say, "I want to be slim and attractive" - it is not the goal. If the result is achieved, you will not keep it for a long time without understanding why you needed it in the first place. Here is an example, in summer, the motivation to lose weight is to attract attention of the opposite sex and to feel more comfortable in open summer clothes. Many women and men can drop a few kilos before the beach season, but then they easily gain their weight back. The answer is very simple - the goal has not been specifically set, and the motivation "has worked" only for a short period of time.

The goal must be clear, specific, motivating and inspiring, so that every time you think of your goal, your pulse rate increases and your heart trembles! This is the real purpose and motivation, and thus, your weight loss process will not be boring and useless.

I suggest that you should answer the first question:

Irina Ahnland

Why do I want to lose weight? Please write down your answer.

....
....

Now the following questions:

How many kilos do you want to lose? Please do not give a quick answer, taking into account your age, constitution and state of your health. Please write down your answer.

....
....

What would these dropped kilos change?

....
....

What changes will take place in my life when I lose weight?

....
....

What will I gain and what I will lose?

....
....

Please write your answers. We will soon work with these notes.

To develop strong and permanent motivation in losing weight, you have to see the ultimate result of your work and all the amazing changes that will happen in your life. You don't have to think about how many dress sizes you need to lose, but what is in store for you when you approach your ideal weight. You don't have to think about a hard and time-consuming process of losing weight, but think of a new and exciting life that lies ahead.

I will give some examples of my clients.

John, 37 years old. I really want to lose weight and have a slim body to be a more successful person. My new body will be an integral part of my brand; I'll feel more confident when I work with my customers and partners. My professional success will reflect on other spheres of my life. I have never really thought about it and so I haven't been able to lose weight.

Kate, 33. I am a happy woman, and I'm really lucky with my husband, he loves me very much and supports me in everything. I have never been slim, I lost weight and gained weight, but it did not upset me much. I am always positive in my life and I have a lot of friends. I have wondered about weight loss recently because I want to give a gift to my dear husband and bring a new romantic wave in our relationship. I dream to celebrate my victory in Venice.

Maria, 42 years old. My main motivation to lose weight is my wish to look younger and feel the lightness in my body. If you are fat, you look older than you really are. I want to wear beautiful dresses, as I used to in my youth, and feel attractive again.

Irina Ahnland

These were the examples of other people. I hope you have already set your own purpose and motivation. This will help to get you driven to reach the goal without hesitation, keep it for years to come, and bring some other positive changes in your life.

Chapter 3. Eating disorders or just emotional hunger?

Have you ever had periods of time when you were eating because you were upset or offended, worried or bored? Do you eat the second portion not because you are very hungry, but because you want to feel better with the help of tasty food? Do not be embarrassed to admit that this has happened to you. This is emotional hunger and most of us have ever tried to suppress this hunger with food. If this seldom happens, it is considered to be normal and it doesn't cause any harm. But if it is getting regular and you go to the kitchen to calm down when you are under stress or when you have troubles, it is emotional dependence on food. It makes you overeat, gain extra kilos and it creates bad mood and even depression.

To find out how your nutrition depends on your emotions, ask yourself the following questions:

1. Can you remember a time when you allowed yourself to eat a lot? Were you really so hungry or did you lose control? Did your desire to eat develop suddenly or did hunger develop gradually?

Sudden attacks of hunger usually indicate an emotional cause. True hunger is growing gradually, going through all its stages and begins with a rumbling stomach.

2. When you felt hungry, was your desire to eat unbearable?

Note, if the real physical hunger can wait, the emotional hunger demands immediate food, for example, high-calorie food and big amounts of it.

Irina Ahnland

3. Did you chew food properly or did you swallow everything without distinction during the meal?

Remember, when you satisfy your natural hunger, you do not lose the ability to control the process. This control begins with the selection of products, calm and proper chewing, enjoying your meal and ends when you feel satiated but not over-eating. Emotional hunger knows no satiation. It is characterized by eating all in sight, you cannot control yourself, lose your mind and at this moment you are just obsessed with food. You stop eating only when you feel full, when your stomach is overfilled with the large amount of food.

4. Do you need any specific, but often harmful products or prefer healthy ones?

Remember that the real hunger can be satisfied with any food, but the emotional eating has its own strong preferences. For example, a favourite cake or something very piquant and spicy, etc.

5. After you become completely full, do you get a feeling of guilt?

In fact, the emotional eating is usually associated with the subsequent guilt. You start blaming yourself, give promises never to lose control again. Note, nothing of this kind happens when you eat to satisfy your physical hunger.

6. Now recall, whether you have moments when you overeat to suppress frustration, resentment and fear.

If you answer "yes", this is definitely emotional eating. Physical hunger is in no way related to your emotional state.

7. The last question is ask yourself, how fast do you eat? If you are really hungry, you will literally relish every bit of food you put into your mouth.

If you experience the emotional hunger, you swallow food automatically, without even noticing it: you don't realize you have eaten it all but the plate is empty.

How to deal with emotional hunger?

First, don't try to ignore your emotional problems. Instead, try to do your best to solve them. If you overeat mostly on the weekends, it is likely to be because of boredom. Be active, choose a new and interesting hobby, so that you could devote your spare time and attention to it, spend more time with friends, get acquainted with new people that you find interesting and enjoy their company.

If you overeat when you feel hurt, analyse why someone's words or actions have touched you so much. Try to take the situation easy, philosophically and change your attitude to it. Be positive! Do not punish yourself with food, just because someone has offended you and you were helpless. If you are angry with something, don't pounce on food but try to distract your attention from it. The best thing you can do is to go for a walk in the park, enjoy a fresh breeze and nature's harmony. Walking accelerates metabolism, enriches the blood with oxygen and relieves stress. Even twenty minutes' walk will help you to calm down quickly and cheer up.

Secondly, sleep for at least 8 hours a day. Proper rest will make you less vulnerable to stress and negative emotions.

Thirdly, control your nutrition. Keep a diary where you'll write down your meals' time, the products you eat and your emotional state. Analyse this list after a few days and you will see how much you overeat during the day, and mostly out of habit.

Observe and analyse your mood and make a list of all your emotional states, when you compulsively overeat or eat without feeling hungry. For example, when you are sad and when you are excited (parties, holidays) when you get offended or when you are tired, when you are under stress and absent-minded. Now, describe the state and write down the action, pleasant activity that can replace the luring temptation.

For example:

1. When I am bored, I often go to the kitchen to have a bite.

Your new action: When I'm bored, I turn on music or watch a movie, call a friend just to chat or arrange to meet up for a cup of coffee.

2. When I'm stressed, I eat to calm down and then I lose control.

Your new action: When I'm stressed, I go for a walk or run in the park, go to the fitness centre or work in the garden.

Do not be lazy to compile this list and keep it handy. Every time when you feel emotional hunger, check the list to see what can help you in this specific mood. Give yourself a little time to adopt the habit "No more comfort food" and after a few weeks, you will feel better and less dependent on food.

If you have a desire to swallow something harmful - promise yourself to do it, only after three "healthy" products. For example, eat an apple, carrots, yogurt before the desired chocolate. Usually, this amount of "healthy" products is likely to satisfy your hunger if you were really hungry. It will be easier for you to resist the temptation to eat.

The most important thing is to fill your life with positive emotions and bright colours and then you will not think about your favourite chocolate bar and you won't need a double portion for dinner.

II. Beauty in simplicity.

Chapter 4. Food to avoid and food to enjoy.

Everyone who wants to keep their figure slim and body healthy should know what products cause weight gain. Of course, it's worth reminding you that the body of each person is unique, so there cannot be a unanimous opinion in relation to the products that lead to gaining weight. Nevertheless studies show that there are some basic products that lead to weight gain.

Generally speaking, the products that contain fat are likely to increase your weight. For example, butter or margarine. As a rule, the fat content of these products equals to seventy percent. It would be logical to assume that margarine with less fat content will be less dangerous, but this is not the case. The problem is that in producing margarine, the element contain fats which are chemically processed. It is these fats that make margarine a particularly dangerous products for your figure and your general health. The same mistake concerns vegetable oil. Most people believe that vegetable oil is almost dietary product but its damage is comparable with the damage from animal fats. Harmful fats include refined and most polyunsaturated fats.

If you want to lose weight, be sure to avoid products which contain a lot of harmful trans fats. The typical product of this kind is mayonnaise. The best replacement of this product in your salad will be low-fat sour cream or natural yogurt.

Everyone knows about the benefits of dairy products, but few people are aware of their danger. Most dairy products can lead to weight gain. Of course, first of all, it concerns butter. The fat content of this product usually equals 72%. No less dangerous are fatty cheese and sour cream, but you should not avoid consuming this calcium-rich food altogether after reading this information. In order to reduce the risk of weight gain, you just need to study the product label thoroughly and simply choose the product with lower fat content. Low-fat cheese is the cheese that contains between 7% to 15% fat. By the way, if you can't imagine your live without cheese, try to choose goat's and sheep's cheese varieties. These kinds of cheese are better absorbed by the body because of their enzyme composition.

Don't forget that meat such as beef and pork also has a high percentage of fat. But here you are faced with the dual problem - after all, a healthy organism cannot do without such a good source of protein, so we should not completely refuse consuming this product. To avoid any problems, you should choose the right kind of meat. The most dietary meat is considered to be chicken meat (especially chicken breast), turkey and fish. At the same time, delicacies such as different types of sausages are much more dangerous than even the fattiest meat. In spite of quite low fat content, they contain many other potentially dangerous ingredients. So take care of yourself and choose a good sort of meat.

Rapid weight gain is caused by semi-prepared food (food you purchase that comes in a can, box, or other package) - Bologna, Hot dogs, Canned pasta, Package Lunch Meats, Chicken Nuggets and other fast food. One should avoid such products altogether. By the way, ready-to-eat so-called healthy breakfast cereals are not, in fact, healthy at all because they are made from already processed products, which make their benefit equal zero. Besides, they are harmful to your health because they are filled with harmful carbohydrates like large amounts of sugar or artificial substitutes.

Fried food makes you gain weight and, moreover, it contains carcinogens that accumulate in the body, and in the long run, it can lead even to blood-vessel occlusion. The most harmful product of this kind is potato chips.

Sweets lead to easy and quick weight gain. Chocolate is the first on this list. Then comes ice cream, different cream cakes and pastries. An interesting fact is that most women are likely to eat sweets when they are under stress and depression. However, I recommend you to eat dried fruit snacks in this situation.

Any alcoholic and carbonated beverages are very dangerous for your figure. Different fruit juices have incredibly large amount of sugar. If you are determined to lose weight, make sure to give up drinking a lot of sweet coffee and sweet tea as well. Carbonated drinks represent a concentration of evil for people suffering from being overweight. They contain so much sugar that the numbers are simply terrifying. As far as alcohol is concerned, apart from containing a large number of calories, it stimulates strong appetite. In fact, red dessert wine contains especially high amount of calories.

What food and how much one should eat in order to effectively lose weight and keep it off?

It's time to tell you about an easy, convenient and effective approach to nutrition. Here I have put together clear and simple tips that are easy to follow. They will help you quickly gain confidence and control over your diet. Let's focus only on the four key areas to understand about balanced and healthy food.

These key areas are proteins, carbohydrates, fats and fibre.

Irina Ahnland

Protein is a vital component. Normal human life is impossible without protein - and it's not the fact that protein makes up minimum 20% of body weight. Its importance stems from the fact that it is responsible for a huge number of biological processes in the body. First of all, protein is essential for growth and development, it serves as a construction material for the formation of new cells. Secondly, protein controls metabolism and immunity. If you do not get enough protein, your body will take it out of your muscles and organs.

Protein consists of amino acids and the absence of one amino acid impedes the assimilation of others. So it is vital to eat both animal and vegetable protein. The approximate daily dose is 1.2 grams of protein per 1 kg of body weight (50% - animal, 50% - vegetable).

Products containing animal proteins: beef, veal, lamb, pork, poultry, pork products, fish, ripe cheese, eggs, milk, mild cheese.

Products containing vegetable proteins: spirulina, bee pollen, soya products, beans and legumes, nuts and seeds, sprouted grains.

Carbohydrates can be simple (monosaccharides) and complex (polysaccharides). Simple carbohydrates give the body "fast" energy, being assimilated in the body in a short period of time. At the same time, complex carbohydrates supply the body with energy slowly and steadily.

Simple carbohydrates include various sweets that contain sugar (sucrose), fruit (they contain glucose and fructose) and products of white refined flour.

Complex carbohydrates can be found in different whole grain cereal: oatmeal, buckwheat, rice, brown pasta, potatoes and vegetables.

Complex carbohydrates are much more useful than simple carbohydrates in terms of fat-burning. The fact is that simple carbohydrates drastically increase the level of blood sugar. In response to this, the pancreas intensely releases insulin - the hormone that regulates sugar levels and lowers them. However at the same time, insulin is considered to be a powerful anabolic hormone, that promotes more fat growth than muscle growth. In this case, insulin is simply converting received simple carbohydrates into fat cells. At the same time, complex carbohydrates softly influence fluctuations in blood sugar levels due to the fact that they are absorbed by the body relatively slowly.

It is important to choose the right types of carbohydrates and to take your meal at the right time. In fact, the human body is designed in such a way that it burns energy in the morning more efficiently and faster. So if you're trying to lose weight or keep it at a certain level, it is vital to take food rich in carbohydrates (potatoes, fruits, grains) from morning till 4 pm. In the evening, you should better choose a vegetable salad as your carbohydrates rich dish.

Fats. We know that extra fat is harmful to your health, but this fat itself is very important. Fats provide the body with multifunctional nutrients that help keep blood vessels elastic, feed the brain and nervous system, supply the body with energy, assist in absorption of vitamins A, D, E. Besides, fats are involved in the synthesis of hormones.

Bad fats: butter, high-fat cuts of meat (beef, lamb, pork), chicken with the skin, whole-fat dairy (milk, cream), cheese, packaged snack foods and semi-prepared food.

Good fats: fish, olive oil and sunflower oil, avocados, nuts, seeds. These fats provide your body with essential fatty acids. However, one of the fatty acids - Omega 3- can only be found in oily fish - such as sardines, tuna, mackerel, salmon.

Fibre.

What is it? Fibre is the indigestible part of plant foods and it controls many processes in the body. It passes through the digestive system from the beginning to the end without being digested. Fibre has a unique ability to absorb water (4-6 times its own volume) to form soft, sponge-like mass in the stomach. That is why products containing fibre, cause a feeling of fullness much faster, which in turn prevents overeating.

Fibre helps to optimize the digestive process by stimulating metabolism and providing more rapid excretion of toxins from the body. Fibre-rich diet delivers friendly bacteria into the digestive tract, which helps to minimize the amount of harmful bacteria and keep the internal balance.

Vegetables rich in fibre are: asparagus, broccoli, Brussels sprouts, cauliflower, celery, courgette, cucumbers, garlic, green beans, green peppers, lettuce. Leeks, mushrooms, peas, spinach, sprouted seeds, tomatoes.

Fruits are also an excellent source of fibre, but they contain a lot of sugar (fructose), which your body turns into glucose that can be stored as fat if it isn't used immediately. Almost all vegetables contain little sugar, so it is recommended to increase the share of vegetables and eat only two different fruits a day during your weight loss. The following fruits such as: apples, apricots, cherries, grapefruit, grapes, kiwi, oranges, peaches, pears, pineapples, plums, strawberries and watermelon are considered to be the best source of fibre. You must receive 25 – 35g of fibre a day. Here is an example of the daily diet containing 35 grams of fibre: 4 dried figs (4.5 g), 1 plate of oatmeal (1.6 g), one large tomato (1 g), a portion of green peas (7.4 g), a portion of broccoli (2.6 g), 1 raw mango (3.9 g), 1 pear (4 grams), 2 slices of pumpernickel bread (3 .7 d) A total is 35 grams of fibre.

Please do not forget to control the portion size of your food and do not overeat. To determine the portion, you can use the so-called "hand" method to measure the ratio of fats, proteins and carbohydrates for a balanced diet. The amount of carbohydrates per meal should be equal to the size of your two fists; the right amount of protein is as large as your palm and as thick as your little finger. The amount of fat should be no more than a phalanx of the thumb.

Follow the healthy and balanced diet. That will forever allow you to lose weight without hunger strikes and disruptions.

Love and take care of yourself! Remember, the food you eat is your health that cannot be bought at any price.

Chapter 5. Healthy eating philosophy.

Eat consciously.

We are all born with the ability to understand the internal signals in our body, but as we grow up, under the influence of stereotypes and intensive rhythm of modern life, we stop eating properly. If you learn to listen to your inner feelings and be attentive to your body, you'll learn to distinguish what food is the most favourable for you. Listen to the slightest sensations in your body and recognize the impact of certain food on your body.

Feelings of drowsiness, heaviness or other discomfort are all warning signals that the food is either of poor quality or is intolerant for your body. Overeating is no less harmful. One should limit the food amount and exclude the components that might cause unfavourable impact. If you notice and write down all the sensations that you have during and after your meal and pay attention to the smallest details, subsequently, you will manage to recognize the properties of food and choose your diet.

Learn to distinguish between the real sense of hunger and simple wish to treat yourself to something tasty. Resist the temptation to eat when you are bored, have some time to spare and when you are just encouraged by others. A cup of tea is the best choice for keeping the conversation with your friends going.

First, you have to show self-control and discipline, but then it will become your habit and healthy eating will be your natural way of life.

Eat a little and often.

Many people are used to eating 2-3 times a day, but they manage to consume an almost full daily amount of calories at a time. The point is that the digestion process takes from 2 to 3 hours. Then special hormones that are responsible for appetite stimulation are produced. The more you don't eat, the more hormones are produced. Accordingly, you are eager to eat more than usual when you have the next chance to eat. Often, after a heavy meal, you always feel sleepy almost at any time of the day. But if you eat little and often, the body's energy level will grow naturally and you will start burning the consumed amount of calories. Small servings are digested more efficiently without overloading the digestive tract and help you to keep normal blood sugar levels.

How to learn to eat little but often? To start with, you need to reduce your main meals by 30 percent and between meals always eat some fruit or drink a glass of fresh fruit juice or fruit and vegetable juice.

Consequent to our bad habits, we have stretched our stomachs with large servings and we got used to the feeling of "full stomach" and excessive satiety. Physiologically, our stomach has a volume of no more than 250-300 grams, but a typical serving nowadays ranges from 800 g to 1000 g, sometimes it is up to 1200 g. The secret is that it can be reduced and this process will not take much time as you may think. The main point is to have frequent meals and to cut portion sizes.

Very soon, approximately in about a week, you will notice that you are satisfied with a smaller food volume to feel full. It will be your first victory! Keep the result for a couple of weeks. After 2-3 weeks, reduce the serving by 30 percent and again keep the result stable. This way you can easily lose weight and then control your weight and you'll not feel hungry all day long.

The simpler the dish, the more healthy it is.

Avoid complex dishes that have been processed through many stages (complex salads, split or sandwiched food, proteins and carbohydrates in the same plate, etc.). When you're eating it all together, you get an explosive mix that leads to the accumulation of body fat.

Many people get depressed just when they think that it is necessary to change their diet and when they start limiting their favourite food. There is also a misconception that a light meal is not tasty and going on a diet means "farewell to freedom". In any endeavour your motivation plays a crucial part. Try to take changing your diet as part of some game called "Let's get a Dream body", for example.

Make a little effort and you will discover that light food eliminates heartburn and heaviness in the stomach after eating, it also gives excellent wellbeing and puts you in a good mood. You'll also get to know that the light meal is tasty, and healthy food is made from all your favourite traditional products. The simplest dishes are easy to cook and cooking takes little time. Besides, light meals are an excellent opportunity to take new and well-forgotten old ingredients and learn how to cook to make them tasty. You can even arrange healthy snacks parties for your nearest and dearest without being afraid to gain extra pounds and get problems with digestion.

Enjoy your meal and eat slowly.

Eating fast almost always leads to overeating. This is because your brain can not focus on the process but the aim is to fill the stomach. Unfortunately, a full stomach alone does not automatically create the sense of saturation it takes time for the "satiety" signal to reach the brain. Scientists say that the signal of satisfied hunger comes with 10 minutes delay. That's why it is important to eat your meal as slowly as possible, so that you have time to realize that you're full before overeating.

When you eat slowly, chewing thoroughly and calmly, you will need less food to satiate yourself. Have you watched small children eating? They spend hours sitting at the table and they enjoy every piece, but hurrying parents always urge them and as a result, it takes the child 10-20 minutes to finish the meal.

In order to learn to eat slowly and enjoy your food without gaining extra kilos, you should not eat in front of the TV, the computer or with a book in your hands.

Make eating look and feel like a beautiful ceremony. Set the table beautifully, light the candles and turn on soft music. Imagine that you are in a nice restaurant, surrounded by soft, relaxing atmosphere. You are left alone with the food, and everything else is put off for a while.

Sit down comfortably, relax before you start eating, look attentively at the dish - as if you are about to taste something new, unknown and very delicious. Examine its colour and shape. Breathe in its aroma. Put the piece slowly into your mouth, focusing on your movements. Once the food is in the mouth, put the cutlery away, put your hands on your knees and concentrate on the process of chewing (you can even close your eyes).

What smells, sounds, tastes, textures do you feel? How does the taste change as you continue chewing? Start with one or two pieces, eat with pleasure. You should spend at least 20 seconds or 20-30 chewing movements for each piece. Later, every meal time will be conscious for you and it will bring you real pleasure. Then you just won't be able to eat in a hurry and on the run.

Avoid diets and eat balanced food.

Avoid diets that exclude or drastically reduce the proportion of carbohydrates, fats or proteins, no matter how effective these diets seem. Your body needs all three components: proteins, fats and carbohydrates. Sharp limitation of any of them leads to stress both for your body and for your mind. Remember, when you are on a diet, proteins get burned first, not fat. The body eats itself, consuming its muscle protein reserves. This leads to the fact that your skin loses elasticity and becomes loose, wrinkled and it develops general immunosuppression because antibodies production is reduced without sufficient protein intake.

Eat healthy and balanced meals. Monitor quantitative as well as qualitative food composition. It should include vitamins, and minerals that the body needs, fibre, carbohydrates and, of course, proteins.

Biological and chemical processes in the body are capable of converting carbohydrates into fats, fats can be transformed into carbohydrates, fats and carbohydrates can be obtained as a result of protein processing, but the body cannot transform any substance into proteins. We get proteins mostly only from food. Therefore, your correct and healthy diet should include protein food, vitamins and mineral elements. The daily protein amount for your body is 1.2 g per 1 kg of body weight and 50% the protein have to be of plant (vegetable) origin.

It is necessary for your diet to include more fruits, vegetables and legumes.

Restrict the use of various tinned food, sparkling water that are rich in all kinds of chemical elements and other similar products.

Follow the right drinking regime.

An important aspect of nutrition is the right drinking regime. In the morning, you should drink a glass of warm water about 30 minutes before breakfast. This will help to wake up your stomach and prepare it for eating. During the day, drink plenty of water at the rate of 30 ml per 1 kg. weight.

All metabolic processes in the body occur with water, and it is water that takes away waste products. It is considered that people who don't drink enough water suffer from chronic fatigue syndrome to chronic dehydration. By drinking enough water, you control the digestion and keep normal metabolism, but it also guarantees that you exclude the possibility of overeating. It's important that you should drink half the daily amount of water before lunch.

Tea and coffee are not substitutes for water, on the contrary, they are diuretics and they dehydrate your body.

Avoid carbonated water and carbonated beverages. Carbon dioxide prevents the intense absorption of an element such as calcium in the digestive tract. Please note that excessive consumption of soda in human bones may become brittle. Also, soft drinks may contain up to 10 teaspoons of sugar which is harmful not only to our figures, but also for our health.

Avoid late meals.

Food eaten less than 3 hours before bedtime does not have enough time to be fully digested. While you are sleeping, all the processes in the body as well as digestion slow down, so all the food you eat before bedtime is not digested until morning. This fact could bring serious digestive system disorders. In addition, a late snack will by all means, affect your figure because the body does not burn calories but stores fat.

Why do people eat before going to bed? There can be many reasons. For some people a substantial late dinner is a kind of habit, for others pizza or sandwiches eaten late at night help them to forget about their problems, while others didn't have opportunity to eat properly in the afternoon, so in the evening hunger makes them attack the refrigerator. At first, in order to stop eating before going to bed, you need to eliminate the reasons for late snacking. Eat regularly during the day, find a more effective way of dealing with stress, and gradually you'll get used to not overeating at dinner.

Chapter 6. Detox your body and shed your weight.

Stress, unbalanced diet and fast food, harmful habits, bad environment, the rapid pace of modern life all turn our bodies into a real landfill of wastes and toxins.

As general contamination of the body increases, the person gets more and more diseases, at first, it is fatigue, inclination to colds, headache, allergy then overweight and obesity. In order to make weight loss process more effective, you need to cleanse your body of toxins and waste products. This will give your body the opportunity to work properly and you will feel healthier as if you are 5 years younger because pollution accelerates the aging process twice.

Juicing

Juice therapy effectively cleans the body, energizes it, and enriches it with vitamins and minerals. During juice therapy, your skin, lungs, liver and kidneys work harder and therefore the body quickly clears itself and gets rid of the accumulated toxins. During such cleaning processes, digestive organs have unique physiological rest and after juicing therapy, they start working more efficiently.

Juices contain natural medicinal substances, plant hormones and antibiotics which enhance the immune system, normalize digestion and reduce cholesterol blood level.

Juices can be vegetable and fruit or they can be made of some plant species as well.

The most frequently used ingredients are:

Greens - spinach, lettuce, beet greens, dandelion leaf, parsley, sprouts
Cruciferous vegetables - kale, cauliflower, broccoli, cabbage, Brussels sprouts
Vegetables - celery, cucumber, red bell pepper, tomato
Root vegetables - carrots, beets, sweet potatoes
Fruits - dark grapes, grape fruit, orange, lemon, apple, mango, kiwi,
Herbs - yucca root, fennel, spearmint, peppermint, basil, chili pepper, fresh turmeric root, milk thistle

If you have never detoxified your body system with juices, I recommend you to start with a three-day fast.

3 days juicing detox diet.

During these three days, you should drink from 1 to 1.5 litres of fresh juice. Drink fresh squeezed juice because biologically active substances reach to light and air and quickly lose their nutritional value. I recommend that you drink a glass of juice every 2.5 - 3 hours. Juices can be mixed or not. During these days, you have to avoid black tea and coffee. You can drink green tea without restrictions. Try to have more rest and enjoy the fresh air these days. Choose a pleasant activity at this time to distract your mind from thinking about food and ask your family to support you.

Let me share my personal experience of a 3-day fasting with juices. The first day of juicing is psychologically complex. Lack of meals creates some discomfort and I feel that I restrict myself from something important. So I try these days to do something interesting and treat myself. I even plan these days beforehand so as not to give up. I can go to a cinema or meet my friends, have a manicure or pedicure done in a salon, get reflex therapy or an Indian head massage, take a walk in the park or sit in the garden and read a book. Time flies quickly, my mood gets better because I have presented myself with some pleasant female things and moreover I have given excellent relaxation to my body these days. On the third day, I may feel a little tired and I can let myself stay in bed all day long reading a book or watching my favourite comedy on the DVD player.

Even if you have a very busy lifestyle, please find these three days for yourself. It will not be a "waste" of time, it will be your investment in your health and beauty. You can start the first day on Friday, drink two glasses of juice in the morning and at lunch time you can find a restaurant where fresh squeezed juice is served and order two glasses, and when you get home, you will continue juicing. Take a bath and go to bed early. Talk with your family and friends and ask for their support. Very soon they will be proud of you and maybe you will be able to inspire your partner to join you and have juice therapy together. I promise you, you will have fun!

Here is a sample plan for juicing. You can make up a plan of your own, but choose fruits and vegetables that you like so that you would enjoy the taste of juice. Really, we've got happy and enjoyable weight loss!

7 am. Juice is made of one grapefruit. You can add a little fresh ginger. This drink perfectly cleans the body of toxins and mucus and destroys the pathogenic flora in the intestines.

9.30 am. Apple juice made of ripe apples and carrots in the ratio of 60 to 40 percentages. It will energize you for the day.

12 noon. Orange and kiwi juice is made in the ratio of 80 to 20 percentages. It will fill your body with vitamin C and will lead to further purification.

2.30 pm. Juice is made of some vegetables (cucumber, spinach, carrots) will calm your body down and it will fill it with vitamins and minerals.

5 pm. Apple and mango juice is made in the ratio of 40 to 60. It will lift your spirits and give you energy.

7.30 pm. Carrot-beet-apple juice in the ratio of 50 to 30 to 20. It will help to remove toxins.

10 pm. or before bedtime. "Green juice." Take 2 large green apples, 2 stalks of celery, 8-10 leaves of lettuce. This juice has a calming effect and ensures a deep sleep.

Day 2.

7 am. Juice is made of one grapefruit. You can add a little fresh ginger. Will continue to clean the body of toxins.

9.30 am. Apple and orange juice. Mix equal parts of apple and orange juice.

12 noon. "Green power" juice. Take 1/4 head of cabbage, 2 apples, a stalk of celery. This juice has a delicious taste and it is an excellent source of vitamins.

2.30 pm. Carrot and apple juice is made in equal proportions. This drink will cheer you up and fill with strength.

5 pm. Apple and beet juice. Mix 4 parts of apple juice and 2 parts of beet juice. It is the perfect drink to clean and strengthen the immune system.

7.30 pm. Orange juice. It will help you to recover.

10 pm. or at night. Carrot and celery juice. It is made from 5 carrots, 2 celery stalks and a bunch of parsley. It is an excellent combination before going to bed and it will help you to get deep sleep.

Day 3.

7 am. Juice of one grapefruit. You can add a little fresh ginger. We continue to clean the body of toxins.

9.30. Mango juice. Good mood and lightness is guaranteed!

12 noon. Orange and kiwi juice in the ratio of 80 to 20. It is a source of energy and vitamin C!

2.30 pm. Pineapple and apple juice. It is made from 3/4 pineapple and 2 apples.

5 pm. Orange and apple juice with some ginger. It is made of 2 apples, 2 oranges and a dice (2x2 cm) of fresh ginger. This drink perfectly relieves fatigue.

7.30 pm. Carrot and cabbage juice. Take 6 carrots and 1/4 head of cabbage. This drink will take your evening fatigue away.

10 pm. or at night. Pear juice. It will help you relax before bedtime.

After the three days of fasting, you will feel energy along with inner ecstasy, you'll have better skin condition and better eyesight. You will lose about 1.5 kg of weight, as a rule, this weight doesn't come back. You will also notice that the weight loss will be faster.

Day 4: Start with your favourite light fruit salad, you can eat properly in an hour, but be careful not to overeat. Drink a lot during the day and eat a salad with every meal in order not to lose control of your meals. This rarely happens. My clients observed that after 3 days of juice fasting, their eating habits change. They need less coffee or chocolate, as well as junk food and start to change eating habits in favour of their usefulness.

3 day juices fasting can take place 3-4 times a year.

3 day fruit and vegetables detox diet.

3 days fruit and vegetables detox diet plan is also a very effective way to clean yourself of toxins and prepare your body for effective weight loss. The fruit and vegetable diet is rich in fibre that is not digested in the body, but provides long saturation. Fibre is a great absorbent that absorbs toxic substances in the intestine and thus contributes to their removal from the body. Simultaneously fibre improves intestinal motility, normalizes its operation and cleaning.

To get ready for these days, buy your favourite fruits, green leafy veg and other vegetables, about the rate of 2 kg per day. You can take vegetables and fruits for juice; it's possible to drink at least half a litre a day. You can eat greens, fruits and vegetables. Arrange a heavenly feast for yourself! These fruits, herbs and vegetables can be used separately and in salads, but don't add anything else. For the salad dressing, you can use a small amount of olive oil and lemon juice. You'd better avoid potatoes, grapes and bananas during fasting days - though they are vegetarian, but very caloric food. Dried fruit is also not recommended because most fruits are dried in the oven and they lose their nutritional value and enzymes.

The time between meals should not be more than 2.5 hours, but you have to eat small servings of food that should not exceed 300g. If you suddenly feel hungry, eat an apple or a pear - these fruits must be on hand all day long. You shouldn't fight with your hunger; otherwise you will not make yourself fast the next day. During the day try to drink a lot of still mineral water, herbal tea, drinking water, natural fruit or vegetable juice. Ideal juice should be prepared by you and diluted with water in a ratio of 3:1 (three parts of juice and one part of water). Purchased juices in packages will not do.

If you have a chronic gastrointestinal disease, be careful with raw vegetables and fruits. Chew thoroughly and eat small servings several times a day. Be attentive to your feelings, if you have stomach discomfort, you can have boiled or stewed vegetables for the next meal.

On the fourth day, you can eat vegetables, lean meat and fish. You'd better avoid flour, sweet and fatty food.

The 7 Days Detox Diet.

During the week, you should avoid meat, poultry, all dairy products, sugar, salt and products containing sugar and salt, wheat products, bananas, grapes, potatoes, coffee and tea except green and herbal tea; also don't eat canned and processed food.

You need to drink 2 litres of water a day and 2 glasses of fresh juice made from fruits or vegetables. Your diet should include plenty of fruits and vegetables, some fish (once a day) and whole grains including brown rice.

Here are recommendations how to compile daily menu.

You'd better start breakfast with a glass of fruit or vegetable juice. In 20 minutes you can have fruit for breakfast or make a big bowl of vegetable salad. If that is not enough for you, add a piece of rye unleavened bread

Lunch

You should eat a big serving of salad, 1-2 tablespoons of olive oil or stewed vegetables (cooked with a small amount of oil). After that, you can have a protein or starchy product. For a protein product, you can take 150-200 g of boiled fish or beans or lentil dishes. If you want to eat a carbohydrate meal, you can eat 150-200 g of brown or whole grains rice (barley, millet, oats, rye, spelt).

Dinner

You must drink a glass of juice, better vegetable juice. In 20 minutes, you can eat a large serving of salad (300-400g) and the first course (150-200g) (carbohydrate or protein). The fish is recommended only once a day.

Have dinner before 7 pm. Remember, food eaten later is more difficult to be digested by the body and it often leads to fermentation.

If you feel faint or dizzy, it means your body is actively being cleaned of toxins and waste products. Drink herbal tea or a glass of still mineral water. Relax and take a stroll on the fresh atmosphere.

Choose one of the detoxing programs you like best and feel yourself reborn!

Chapter 7. Happy weight loss diary.

I have noticed from my professional experience that my clients who keep a weight loss diary achieve better results than those who are too lazy to make notes. There are several reasons for

this:

Weight loss diary gives accurate information about the amount of food eating and when you see all this information, you can adjust your diet to achieve the best results.

A weight loss diary is a great motivator. It is your written commitment to yourself to get a slender figure, improve your health and also make your life better and more interesting. Also, the daily display of your results and achievements will be a powerful stimulus to further self-improvement.

Moreover, it is not going to be an ordinary weight loss diary but a Happy Weight Loss Diary. Here we will write down not only your anthropometric data and nutrition information but we will register the positive moments that happened during the day. By the way, you will note the pleasant things you treat yourself during the day. This will help you always to be in a good mood and it will teach you to enjoy every new day. You will find a huge part of your life wonderful and exciting, you'll make the most unexpected discoveries and you'll easily reach your perfect figure.

So how to make Happy Weight Loss Diary

To start with, I recommend you should buy a beautiful and expensive notebook, in fact, you will write down your success, victories and a lot of more interesting things.

Perhaps your diary will be a great legacy for your children, who will find it and say, "Oh, once again, Mom rocked it out!" or" Oh, what a hero our dad is". You will encourage them by your example to the first deeds.

Please write Happy Weight Loss Diary or Magic Weight Loss Diary on the cover of your notebook and date it.

Stick your most favourite and beautiful picture on the first page of the notebook. You can even choose the one where you look much slimmer and younger. The main thing is that you like this picture and it creates a pleasant mood.

Write your ideal weight that you want to achieve and your motivation - why you want to lose weight on the second page. We have been working with this task in the chapter "Let's get started".

I remind you of these questions.

Why do I want to lose weight?

What would these dropped pounds change?

What changes will take place in my life when I lose weight?

What will I get and what will I lose?

Then write your current weight, desired weight and how many kilograms you need to drop.

The next step is to define your intermediate goals for weight loss every 12 weeks. I encourage you to lose weight not by more than 0.5-0.7 kg per week. Please calculate these milestones and date each goal.

For example:

My current weight is 96 kg, the desired weight is 60. I need to lose 36 kg.

My first intermediate goal for the first 12 weeks is 7 kg. Implementation date is March 4.
The second intermediate goal: 7 kg. Implementation date is May 27.
The third intermediate goal: 6 kg. Date: the 5th of August.
The fourth intermediate goal: 6 kg. Date: the 28th of October.
The fifth intermediate goal: 6 kg. Date: the 27th of January.
The ultimate goal: 4 kg. The date of its implementation is on March 31. Hooray!

If you go ahead of your intended plan, it is fine, just adjust the date. But please, be realistic and do not rush. Weight loss is often rapid in the beginning and it is slower in the second phase. If this happens to you, be patient and be pleased with each half a kilo that you drop in a week. Again I repeat - 0.5 kg per week is the most optimal and healthy weight loss.

On the next page draw the following table:

Date						
Week	1	2	3	4	5	6
Weight						
Waist						
Thigh						
Hip						
Bust						
Upper arm						

Each week write down your morning weight and body measurements.

Take a few more pages to continue this table and then the most interesting thing happens ...

In the following pages, real magic will begin.

You put the date on the top of every page.

When you're going to eat something, first write it down in your happy weight loss diary and only then start your meal. This point is the most difficult and it is especially important for those who have tried to lose weight many times without any result.

Write down the amount of liquid you drank during the day and your small snacks between meals. Please, choose healthy snacks.

Now the most unusual!

Every day, you should treat yourself to three pleasant things. They do not necessarily have to be large and significant, they may even be very simple, but they are so desirable to you that it will bring happiness for the whole day. Ability to experience joy is the greatest ability that a person has. All we need is to draw your attention to something that brings joy and keeps that feeling. The most important thing is that the joy accompanies you every day and over time it will become your natural state.

You'd better plan this joy beforehand, before going to bed, think how you will be able to express love and please yourself. Good mood in the morning will be guaranteed and you'll think first not about your problems, endless work and troubles but your three pleasant things that will make your new day colourful.

But that's not all. You also need to write funny stories, amazing events and subtle dramatic moments in your diary.

For example, this is a page from Maria's diary who is one of my clients:

Date: January 30, 2012

Morning weight: 70 kg

Before breakfast: a glass of mineral water

Breakfast: sugar-free cereal with skimmed milk, 1 banana, coffee without sugar.

After breakfast - 2 glasses of water, 1 apple.

Lunch: vegetable soup with lentils, bran cereal, spinach salad, tea with milk

After lunch: three glasses of mineral water, 1 cup of coffee.

Dinner: Salmon with rice and vegetables, tea

Before going to bed: half a glass of yogurt.

My three pleasant things:

• I put on a beautiful blouse and went to the office. At work, my colleagues asked me what the important event was. Actually, I have every day an important event recently.

• I bought tickets for the operetta Carmen. I am going to watch it with my friend really, I have not asked her if she would like to go.

Irina Ahnland

• I've bought flowers to please myself.

My current positive moments:

This day was sunny and surprisingly warm though it is January.

The chief praised my latest project at work. Maybe it was because of the beautiful blouse?

The smile has never left my face most of the day.

As you begin to write Happy Weight Loss Dairy, you will appreciate its importance and you will see the result from the very first day. This diary will be your friend and weight loss coach. You will soon see yourself from a different perspective and you will realize very soon that you are a strong and successful person and you can cope with everything.

Chapter 8. Turn your bad eating habits into good ones.

It is food that unites all of us, regardless of gender, age, nationality and religion. Our body is designed so that the most important elements are obtained from food. We can change one diet concept after the other, restrict ourselves to certain food and even fast from time to time, but to completely abandon food is not in our power. A balanced diet is as necessary for people as the air breathed in daily and also food is one of the main essentials and common addictions we acquired from childhood.

Our eating behaviour is as a result of eating habits that we have inherited for a long time. What is a habit and food habit in particular? It is a way of behaviour that becomes a necessity. There are certain behaviour programs which always "work" in certain circumstances.

These wrong food habits that largely determine our problems with being overweight, and we experience great difficulties when we start following a new weight loss program in an attempt to change our eating behaviour. It is not easy to change existing habits, which take a lifetime to form; so these habits have become an integral part of us and therefore we must work constantly and persistently in order to change them.

The most well-known negative habits for a slim figure:

1. No breakfast.
2. Habit of eating as you go.
3. Eating in front of the TV.
4. Late meals.
5. Drinking little water.

6. Snacks instead of normal meals.
7. Quick meals.
8. Big intervals between meals.
9. Habit of eating large portions.
10. Overeating due to stress.

Please, list your bad eating habits that prevent you from being beautiful. If you have any habits from the list above, write them below and if you have any other personal habits, please add them to your list. You will need it soon for work.

1 ....

2 ....

3 ....

Let me congratulate you on your courage and determination. I bet that your list is interesting and impressive, so what shall we do with this heavy luggage on our way to a slim figure?

Choose one habit from the list that you intend to work on and write it in your Happy Weight Loss diary. Psychologists believe it takes 21 days to get rid of the old habit, and of course, their forecasts are likely to be naive. Nevertheless, let's try it. During the next 21 days, you must repeat one and the same action. Please reconsider your day schedule and make a plan of action. Take your diary and describe these 21 days in detail, write everything you will do for your beloved body. Isn't it one of the most important things to do?

Be decisive, positive, have faith in the result and a little passion. Evaluate the importance of the challenge of your task. After all, such a harmless looking habits affect the quality of your life, your inner state and appearance. This habit is absolutely useless for you. It's high time to say goodbye to this habit and get a new and useful habit instead. Now you enjoy everything good!

Here are advice and some tips below to get rid of the most common bad eating habits; Do not forget about the deadline - when you're going to challenge your habits and when you are going to celebrate your victory over this habit. You can even make notes in a funny way, for example:

Mission to eliminate bad habits of No breakfast!

Starting mission -29 April 2014
End of mission -19 May 2014

Evaluate your feelings after 21 days. If you don't find any traces and memories of this bad habit, you can congratulate yourself with success. I even suggest celebrating this important event! Imagine the way you can impress your friends and inspire them with your example. In fact, now that you have breakfast in your diet, you feel better, get less tired, go to work with a smiling face and you have even lost a couple of extra kilos. Just think, now your friends will go to work with smiling faces!

Please, don't acquire any other new bad habits while celebrating this event.

What do you do if the habit still persist or relapse from time to time? The answer is simple - keep working on courageously. Once again, give yourself another 21 days, as psychologists would advise, but let's use more strategic and more sophisticated methods. Remember to mention in your notes that the Mission continues ...

1. No breakfast.

When people are in a hurry to work or school in the morning, they often skip breakfast, taking only a cup of tea or coffee. According to researchers, no breakfast in the long run leads to a slower metabolism, develops gastrointestinal and cardiovascular diseases and, as a consequence, weight gain. People who do not eat breakfast tend to overeat during the day, unlike those who have breakfast. Therefore, if you want to lose weight and keep the desired weight off, please arrange a proper and healthy breakfast.

Tip:

Select for breakfast anything that you like best, which is good, healthy and easy to cook. If you have no appetite in the morning, have a small portion of food. In the evening, it is better to plan your breakfast in advance so that in the morning you can easily and quickly cook it. Get used to getting up earlier - so that you could enjoy your breakfast and meet the day with the most joyful expectations.

2. Habit of eating as you go

Eating as you go is harmful because, as a rule, you don't pay enough attention to the quality of food you eat. You can get a stomach ache, bloating and heartburn, overeating and extra kilos as a result. Every food you eat as you go is not usually healthy.

Tip:

If, for any reason, you cannot afford a proper meal, please take bananas, apples, almond nuts or healthy snack with nuts and whole grains without sugar.

One medium-size ripe banana is a wonderful snack option during the day. It contains only 110 calories without fat and cholesterol; rich in potassium which is good for heart and vitamin B6 for the nervous system. Apples also perfectly satisfy hunger, they are a source of vitamin C, antioxidants and fibre.

Almonds are very good for health. They can be a great choice of good snacks, they are considered to be a source of protein, polyunsaturated and monounsaturated fats that satisfy hunger and prevent overeating. Moreover, almonds are useful for brain and heart; they normalise blood pressure, cholesterol level and increase energy.

Healthy snacks with nuts and whole grains are rich in protein, complex carbohydrates and fibre. They will help you to satisfy your hunger and make the diet more balanced. Please, mind your quantity. One bar is usually enough for a bite.

3. Eating in front of the TV

Nutrition specialists found out that as a result of eating while watching TV, a person is likely to have an extra 300-350 calories. The fact is that while watching TV, we focus almost all our attention on watching the screen. We distract our attention from eating and our brain does not have time to signal that the stomach is full. Thus, mindless eating leads to overeating. We also risk getting problems with digestive tract, while watching TV; we often eat fast, swallowing large pieces of food.

Tip:

Eat properly before watching TV and you may take nutritional drinks - juice, smoothie, herbal tea during TV times. This is another step to a slim figure!

4. Late meal

Eating time is very important for the figure. It does not matter if you are an "owl " or an " early bird because if you have dinner after eight in the evening, you risk gaining weight. Late and a large dinner, containing a lot of fat and protein may also affect the quality of sleep. For the "processing" organs, the night becomes the "night of horror", and our dream is distorted and not smooth.

Tip:

After 8 p.m., the digestive tract slows down, digestibility of food reduces and the waste removal becomes more difficult. This leads to the body intoxication and may even contribute to the accumulation of salt and stones in kidneys and bladder. As a rule, a late dinner causes overeating.

Try to have dinner not later than 7-8 p.m. Choose low-fat protein food and vegetables to follow. Eat slowly, with pleasure.

5. Drinking little water

Water is an indispensable element in our live, besides, it is necessary for efficient nutrients absorption and burning calories. The amount of water in the human body ranges from 50-70%. Even our bones contain one-third of water. Losing at least one tenth of the body water is very dangerous.

Insufficient water intake leads to too much workload for our kidneys, which have to work with more intensity to output more toxins with a minimum amount of water.

Tip:

Make it a rule to drink at least 1.5-2 litres of water a day or 30 ml per 1 kg of body weight to be exact. Quality water or still mineral water should be preferred to any other type. The appropriate water intake is 15 minutes before eating or 2-2.5 hours after eating. By taking water during meals, you dilute the gastric juice and the food is not completely digested.

Develop the habit of drinking water by setting a reminder on your phone or using a timer. You can pour your daily amount of water in a two-litre bottle or a jug. It will be a visual reference of how much water you drink a day. Put a glass of water on your table and as soon as it is empty, fill it up with water again. Always carry a water bottle on a daily basis.

Start your day with a glass of clean water. Add some good mood to the water and wish yourself a good day!

6. Snacks instead of meals

This habit can lead to obesity and stomach illnesses, especially when snacking starts displacing normal meals. You lose control over the amount of food you eat, as well as the quality of food. The reason for snacking may be a desire to cheer up. When at work, on the way home or if you feel tired, you take a chocolate, sandwich or chips as a snack. You feel a little better, but not for a long time, because such food has no nutritional value and it only rewards you with empty calories.

Irina Ahnland

Tip:

To keep the body in good shape and avoid starvation, you should accustom yourself two snacks during the day. Instead of cookies or chocolates, it's better to eat an apple or a banana, a handful of nuts or other dried fruit, a small salad or a small pot of yoghurt. Plan your meals carefully and always take a healthy snack, in case you want to have a bite.

7. Quick meal

Since childhood everyone knows that food should be chewed thoroughly and slowly, but not all of us follow this simple rule.

The habit of eating quick is harmful both for health and body. Let's talk about health first. The digestion process begins when chewing. Do not get surprised! The further digestion process depends on the way you chewed food, and if you don't chew well enough and swallowed large pieces, all the digestive organs have to work harder to correct our badly chewed mistake. The habit of eating quick just wears out the digestive system and, as a result, the food is not fully absorbed by the body. Having not been absorbed, this food will turn into toxins that cause weight gain, skin rashes and other unpleasant consequences.

Tip:

To get rid of this habit, make yourself eat slowly and chew thoroughly. Take as little pieces of food as possible, chew them slowly, enjoy the food and the process of eating. Enjoy the pleasant taste and mouth-watering look of the dishes. Chew every bite at least 25-30 times. This will give your stomach enough time to properly digest the nutrients. This way, the sense of saturation comes faster and you will feel full for a long time and the stomach walls will not be stretched with too much food. Over time, you will notice that your portion size is considerably reduced, probably, as well as your clothes size.

8. Big intervals between meals

Surprisingly, big intervals between meals do not make the waist thinner and the figure slimmer. Quite the contrary, the body starts saving energy and slowing metabolism. That is where stubborn extra weight comes from. On the one hand, you do not eat a lot, but still you do not get slimmer. The kilos stick tight to the body.

Talking about health, long intervals between meals lead to stagnation of gall and formation of stones in the gallbladder, not to mention stomach diseases. Let's not create such painful work conditions for vital organs but take good care of our health.

Tip:

Try to follow the diet and avoid long intervals between meals. It's better to eat less but more often. The optimal time interval between meals is from 3 to 4 hours. Remember your happy childhood: you had a happy breakfast, a happy lunch, a happy dinner, a very happy afternoon tea and a cheerful dinner.

Our food brings not only nutritional benefits but also the pleasure, so it is important to plan a good and joyful diet. If you have a busy schedule, you'd better prefer healthy snacks. Fruit and berries, nuts and dried fruit, a small glass of delicious yogurt, fruit salads will improve your mood and increase your energy for the rest of the day.

9. Habit of eating large portions

The habit of eating large portions directly leads to overeating and consumption of extra calories, which are later stored on the waist and hips. Furthermore, large food volumes stretch your stomach and so you quietly get used to large food portions to feel comfortable and satisfy your appetite. Such habit can eventually lead to the digestive system disorder and organism intoxication. Thus, in addition to extra kilograms, you can acquire chronic fatigue, apathy, unhealthy complexion or skin rash.

Before you blame yourself for gluttony, let's see what should be the right size of food portions. To describe the proper portions, we will use our fists and hands as the units of measurements. The stomach of every person has the volume of two fists. Thus, at every meal, one shouldn't consume more than this amount of food. There are some guidelines that you should follow when eating. These rules are as follows:

1. The right portion of vegetables and vegetable dishes is equal to two fists.
2. One serving size of fresh fruit that you should eat at a time is about one fist. (Consumption of a lot of fruits at a time can cause their fermentation, bloating and digestive system disorder).
3. One meat portion is a piece that has the size of your palm.
4. Bakery products and pasta, as well as cereals, beans should have a volume of no more than one fist.
5. The serving size for low-fat dairy products is 1 palm.

Such information seems to be unbelievable and even funny, doesn't it? The portions in restaurants and cafes offer other standards; plenty of sandwiches that are displayed in shops are of giant sizes. Indeed, over the last 20 years, the size of food portions has increased significantly. Ancient sages encouraged us to eat in order to live, whereas modern food industry promotes another slogan. We live to eat, turning us into consumers.

Tip:

First and foremost, give yourself time and be patient. Start eating small food portions gradually, with comfort and pleasure. Change your plates to a smaller size, and also try to find small spoons, knives and forks. The colour of plates also affects our mood and appetite. Bright colours (orange, yellow, red) stimulate appetite, whereas calm colours (grey, blue and green colours) suppress it. If you're wondering what colours, follow Feng Shui advice for regulating appetite , then I want to share with you the following tip: white plates are the best choice , as white symbolizes discipline , rules and moderation.

Set the table beautifully, creating a special mood. Put the amount of food you feel comfortable on your new plates but this amount is sure to be less than you used to have. Why not remove one spoonful of food from the plates and add a few leaves of lettuce instead. Consume the food slowly with pleasure, enjoy the smell of food and be glad with every piece that you take. The next day, replace another spoonful of food with beautiful lettuce leaves and then day by day gracefully reduce your food portion spoon by spoon.

Follow your feelings and avoid any discomfort. If you feel that you need time to get used to a new portion size, allow your body to stick to the initial result for few days or a week. Ideally, your portion size should consist of an amount of food that may fit in your cupped palms. When you reach this result, you will stop dreaming about large and cheerful heaps of food that you could hardly imagine your life without some time before.

10. Overeating due to stress

Some people influenced by stress or emotions completely lose appetite, and some people get as hungry as a wolf and they eat a huge amount of high-calorie food as distress mechanism for a while. The food in these cases acts as a drug that helps them to doze off and relax. Indeed, they get better for a while, but not long. The food has already been eaten, but the problems still remain and besides, people are frustrated about having overeaten due to stress. Negative experience is accompanied by another fresh negative experience and the next emotional overeating. It's a vicious circle and overweight begins growing rapidly.

Tip:

I have written in detail about compulsive overeating in Chapter 3 "Eating disorders or just emotional hunger". Please refer to this chapter, read it several times and follow the given advice. The main thing is not to fight with yourself. If you feel like eating in the moment of stress, that's how your body works, you'd better eat something, let it be not high-calorie food but something useful. For example, a big bowl of fruit salad or a lot of fruit at one time, but it will be another choice, more healthy and conscious one. Herbal tea helps to control appetite and calm down. Keep herbal tea always at hand. Drink a cup of herbal tea before a meal, and a little tea during the meal. I have noticed that green tea has a wonderful ability to reduce excessive appetite.

Please, do not stay alone. Ask your nearest and dearest ones to support you and this will be the best thing you can do for yourself. Let them know that they can always rely on you as well, even when they are just in a bad mood. Appreciate your friendship and take care of your dear friends.

Other eating habits

If you have any other eating habits on your list, I advise you to ask yourself the following questions and write down the answers.

1. How often does this habit take place in your life?

....
....
....

2 . Can you remember when it appeared and why?

....
....
....

3 . What do you feel before and after eating?

....
....
....

4. Will you find any way to distract your attention and avoid this habit - call a friend, go for a walk, in general, to switch to something positive, not related to food? Write down your answers.

....
....
....

5. Can you find a way to transform a bad habit into a good one for your health and beauty? Write down your answers.

....
....
....

Now write down all the ideas and actions that you decide to take to gradually get rid of this nutty habit in favour of other more useful habit.

1..
2..
3..
4..
5..

Only remember to give yourself 21 days, as psychologists recommend for the habit to lose its power and "weight", and you, by the way, could lose weight too. Make a note in your diary of the date you start working on this habit and the date of its "Saying goodbye".

Be sure about your victory and visualise your attractive freedom - your new quality of life and your new image!

If this habit is so unique that it has managed to survive after 21 days, give yourself another 21 days for the job, and do not forget to tell us about your experience. We will be glad to get psychologists puzzled.

Part III. The law of attraction for weight loss.

Chapter 9. Creative visualisation.

Creative visualisation is a very powerful weight loss tool. The proverb says: "A picture is worth a thousand words." The subconscious mind can be influenced by both words and images. Words are involved in affirmations whereas images stand for visualisation. When we visualise our desires, we simply run the film script in our mind and if you visualise according to the laws of visualisation, you help your body shed weight.

Our subconscious mind accepts and perceives mental images as real. Visualising yourself with a perfect shape as you want to see yourself, you program your subconscious mind to rebuild your body as precise as possible according to the mental image.

Why not use the connection between your mind and body to create wonders? Our thoughts and emotions affect the body condition. Negative thinking, stress, anxiety, fear or anger have a negative impact on your mental and physical health. Positive thinking, joy, love, harmony and trust heal and fill the human body with force and energy. Visualise your body the way you want it to be, leave your doubts and other negative thoughts and focus on what you're doing.

In any business, you need patience and persistence. You can do a short visualisation for a few minutes several times a day or practise longer visualisation at bedtime. During short visualisation, I would recommend you to imagine yourself as a beautiful person with ideal weight. Please, do not worry

Irina Ahnland

about your present appearance. After all, it's only temporary! Create a new reality in your imagination and fill yourself with positive feelings.

The traditional method of visualisation consists three steps:

1. Relaxation.
2. Creating an image of the future.
3. Emotional delight.

1. First, you need to attain a state of relaxation. Close your eyes, take a breath and slowly breathe out. Allow your body to gradually enter the relaxation state. Feel that your legs, back, chest, stomach, arms, shoulders, neck, face are relaxing... Your mind quiets down. You are well.

When you have reached the desired state, proceed to the second stage.

2. Imagine your desired image on a mental screen. You can even think of your little action script, the image of your Future, the Beautiful and Gorgeous self or use the following script.

Imagine that your wish has come true. Start with the physical sensations. Where are you and what you're doing? What do you feel? What do you hear? What do you see? Keep this state for a few minutes. Then start adding details to this image, everything that you think are important and meaningful for you. Enjoy every moment of this process!

3. The next step is filling your visualisation experience with emotions. Feel maximum joy that YOU did it! YOU have reached YOUR goal! Now you fully enjoy what's going on in your life! It was YOUR big dream and it came true. You are

celebrating YOUR victory and this event is one of the most delightful and wonderful experience.

So, these are a few ideas to work with visualisation.

• Imagine yourself standing in front of a full-length mirror with a perfect figure - slim and fit. Admire your hair and make-up (for females). Look how beautiful and elegant your clothes are. Look at yourself on all sides. Turn around in front of the mirror and touch your small waist and perfect hips. Your body is now the ideal size, beautiful and bouncy, as you've always dreamt of!

• Draw in your imagination the desired numbers on the scale. Imagine yourself standing on the scale and pleased to notice your new result. Congratulate yourself on the victory over excess weight. Have a tremendous time with your new shape! Now you have something to be proud of – a slim and fit shape.

• Imagine that you are lying on a beautiful beach, and the weather is sunny and warm. Just see how well and harmonious you look in your swimming suit. Well, where is your extra weight then? I believe that you need to get up and walk proudly with such gorgeous body. Okay, well, you just got up to buy yourself some refreshing ice juice.

• Imagine that you put on the clothes that you have always wanted to wear. It's time to forget the phrase "This is not for me." Only the most beautiful, stylish and elegant clothing is now for you and the mirrors in the dressing rooms surround you with love and delight as never before.

• Visualise the celebration in a cosy and luxurious restaurant where you invited your family and close friends. You are the host of the party and the reason for such an event is your new luxurious body! Have fun, joke, enjoy yourself with your friends and celebrate your victory! Catch their admiring glances and take a lot of their compliments. Feel like it's happening now and not in the future. If you love to dance, then dance for your friends and give them one more surprise. Now imagine that every person is coming up to you one by one, presents you flowers or a gift and says to you their most sincere and warm words. You simply shine with happiness and thank them for all their love and support. Stay in this state for a while to feel the joy and the euphoria of the fulfilment of your dreams!

Create any scene you want in your mind. Fill it with colours, emotions and sensations. Let the action of the scene be interesting, lively and intriguing. Look at yourself in every scene, as if you've lost weight, look younger and started a new happy life.

End the session by visualising a positive attitude and pleasant emotions. If you have any thoughts of doubt, simply do not contemplate them and they will soon stop coming to you. Let the thoughts of beauty, joy and harmony occupy your mind.

Develop your imagination and dream. Create yourself and your life as a work of art!

Chapter 10. The secret of positive affirmations.

Affirmations are positive statements that help us to change the way of thinking and create the future that we desire.

Affirmations are thoughts, words and emotions that each of us uses in everyday life and unfortunately we do not only use positive but also negative statements.

If you wish to get a slim figure and beauty, you need to learn to control your thoughts, learn to think and talk about yourselves and your bodies only in a positive way. All our thoughts and emotions create our lives and everything that surrounds us. Positive emotions attract positive events in our lives, negative thoughts attract negative events. Everything we think about becomes a part of our live.

The first thing that you need to pay attention to is the way you speak and what you say. Secondly, train yourself to replace all the negative thoughts that come to you with the positive ones, and if suddenly you say something about yourself in the negative manner, immediately correct yourself. It's not difficult, all you need is to focus and be patient. For example, if you often tell yourself, "Well, I've just put on some weight,» replace this phrase with "It's OK. I'll easily get in shape."

Now I would like to tell you in details how to make your affirmation really effective.

First of all, the affirmation must be made only in the affirmative form that is it is prohibited to use the negatives "no", "not", "never" in the statement. It is considered that our subconscious mind simply ignores the "not", so affirmation made with a "not" works against us. <u>For</u>

example, if you say "I will never lose weight," it will be really hard to lose weight with this statement.

When you pronounce the affirmation, you should imagine that your dream has already come true. That is, the statement must be written in the present tense. If you say "I will lose weight by the New year's day," your subconscious mind understands that you are going to lose weight some year but when exactly. Unfortunately, your mind doesn't understand such a statement. The subconscious mind simply does not perceive the words "tomorrow", "will" or "in the future." It is better to say "I'm slim, I've lost weight." Affirmations should be short, about 5 words ideally. If your affirmations are over 10 words divide them into two smaller affirmations.

Make an affirmation that brings you positive and pleasant emotions. The stronger the emotions, the more effective your affirmation will be. In other words, use colourful words such as "incredible", "cool", "gorgeous", "wonderful", etc. For example:

I have a gorgeous body!

I always look amazing!

How wonderful, I'm losing weight so easily!

And if you add the word "love" to your affirmations, they will simply be magical for you and it won't take you long to see the result.

I love and appreciate myself!

I love my beautiful body!

I love taking care of myself!

I love my new healthy lifestyle!

I love myself and my life!

You should repeat the affirmations frequently, otherwise they will not work. Be patient and spend less time analysing your old beliefs and mistakes. They all have become your history; so what is the need to waste your time? Many wonderful things are in store for you, so be ready to welcome this miracle right now.

Here is a list of effective affirmations that you can use as well.

• I start the day with joy every day.
• I take good care of my body each day.
• My body is getting stronger and slimmer every day.
• I look younger and feel lighter with each passing day.
• I have a perfect weight.
• I have a perfect body.
• All the cells of my body are working together in perfect harmony.
• I choose healthy and nourishing food.
• I look great and I feel great in my favourite clothes.
• I enjoy keeping my ideal weight.
• It is easy and effortless to lose weight.
• Every day I look slimmer and feel happier.
• I exercise with joy and purpose.
• Losing weight simply comes naturally and easy to me.
• Every day I am getting slimmer and healthier in every way.

Chapter 11. Treasure map – manifest your dreams!

Have you ever dreamt of finding a treasure map and then start a breath-taking journey? Everyone in childhood has dreamt of finding a real treasure – a buried treasure chest or at least a purse with a few coins to buy an ice cream. Growing up, we become more serious and we live with the belief that miracles happen only in fairy tales.

But life can really become a wonderful fairy tale that is full of wonders, magic and dreams coming true. In order to participate in this fairy tale, you need a treasure map or Bagua Treasure Map to be exact. Treasure Map is the most amazing and beautiful way to achieve goals.

A Treasure Map will not only help you lose weight and transform you, but it will also improve all areas of your life, because it has different " sections " for wealth , career, creativity, health, love, etc. This means that it cannot simply fulfil one wish but improve all your life. If you don't believe it - just try it and you will be pleasantly surprised!

A Treasure Map often looks like a big square divided into 9 equal-sized smaller squares, where you place pictures or photos symbolising your desires or dreams in a certain order. You can also find a map representing an octagon or a rectangle, but I would recommend you to make a square treasure map. The basis of this card is Feng Shui Bagua technique "Eight life aspirations". That is why the Treasure Map is so effective, it unites both wisdom of Taoist philosophers and applied psychology.

The layout and meaning of the sectors of the Bagua map are as follows.

Wealth, Prosperity, Self-Worth	Fame, Reputation and Social Life	Love, Relationship, Marriage
(southeast)	(south)	(southwest)
Colours: purple, green, gold.	Colours: red.	Colours: pink, skin tones, earth tones.
Family	Health, Harmony, Beauty	Children, Creativity and Entertainment
(east)		
	(centre)	(west)
Colours: purple, green, gold.	Colours: yellow, earth tones.	Colours: white, bright.
Wisdom, Self-knowledge and Self-Cultivation	Career, Life mission and Individuality	Travel and Helpful People
(northeast)	(north)	(northwest)
Colours: blue-green.	Colours: dark, blue, black.	Colours: grey, mauve

Now let's get down to the most interesting part and see how to create a treasure map.

So, you will need a sheet of drawing paper, coloured paper, scissors, glue, coloured pens, markers, a pencil, an eraser, a ruler, blue tack. But the most important components of the map are pictures and images of your desires, goals and dreams.

You can buy the office supplies at your local office supply store. I wish you to go shopping in a good mood smiling mysteriously. I bet that on seeing you, the shop assistants will be very glad to help you with your shopping list, because they are used to meeting exhausted students or hopelessly serious accountants.

Your next task is to find some time and stay alone to think and dream about all aspects of your life. Equip yourself with a pen and a sheet of paper. It's time to use it.

Let's start with the basic and central sector - Health, Beauty and Harmony.

Visualise yourself having perfect weight, being beautiful or handsome (for men), full of life, joy and health. Have you seen it? It's great, isn't it? Please, write down your affirmations.

For example: I am beautiful and harmonious. I have a strong and well-built body (for men). My weight now is ... (please put your ideal weight). I love myself and my life! I enjoy every day and every moment of my life!

In this sector, you will need to find your favourite photograph where you look happy, pretty, younger and slimmer. Let it decorate your treasure map and make it a centre focus!

Wealth and prosperity sector

This sector is responsible for everything that has to do with money, prosperity and abundant wealth. Please think, how much money you want to attract into your life? What is your salary or business income? Write down your answer. For example, my monthly salary is (amount).

If you want to attract prosperity and material abundance, think about it and play with your imagination. If you want to dream big, please do. But do not forget that large desires require more time. Next, you will need to find a picture or an image that symbolises your desire. This can be your new salary cheque or an image of banknotes with big denominations to attract financial luck for your business. In general, it can be anything that you consider to be the personification of wealth and prosperity and feel free to express your sense of humour.

It is in this sector where you can settle your dreams of a new car, a house or an apartment, expensive furniture, diamonds. Enhance this sector with your affirmations. The affirmations may be as follows: " I'm driving a new car ", " we are giving a house-warming party in our new house on 10.07.2019."

Fame, Reputation and Social Life Sector

This sector helps to achieve success and recognition in society. Visualise yourself being recognised in the area that you plan. If you want to become a public figure, imagine yourself on the stage being congratulated, awarded a diploma, grant or reward. Maybe you see yourself giving a seminar or a presentation. Probably you are being interviewed for a popular magazine or a TV program. Or maybe you are surrounded by a crowd of fans or followers?

Some extra images of medals and cups will effectively enhance this sector.

If you are not focused on social recognition and you have different values, just think about your talents being recognised by your family, friends and acquaintances. Probably, you can cook perfectly, crochet beautifully or you are talented interior designer and decorator. These are not less special talents than public speaking or writing scientific papers. Are they?

In this sector, you can also place images of famous people you admire at the moment of being awarded or the highest points in their fame.

Love and Relationship Sector

This sector is responsible for marriage and the sphere of relationships. If you are married or you already have a relationship, choose one of your favourite photos, where you are together. You can write below the affirmation about your harmonious and happy relationship with your partner. It will enhance the sector.

If you have no relationship yet, find a picture or an image that you consider to symbolise of love, romance and joy. Lots of ideas for decorating this sector are available on Valentine's Day postcards. You can also take pictures of two hearts and doves, remember about affirmations stating that you are very happy, you love and being loved.

Health and Family Sector

You want all of your family to be happy and healthy, don't you? Fine. So you will need a photograph of your family members where they look happy and harmonious. You can even create the necessary affirmation at once.

You can do it in another way. Make a photo collage where you look beautiful (or handsome), happy and slim (well-built) and your family happily and solemnly celebrates your successful transformation and weight loss. You can also create your personal affirmations or add the following affirmations:

My family is so proud and so happy for my weight loss result.

I am very thankful for all support and encouragement they have given to me.

Children, Creativity and Entertainment Sector

It is the sector of joy, excitement and wonder. If you dream of children, place an image of a cute boy or a girl, or twins to surprise everybody. It really works! I know two wonderful examples from my acquaintances.

If you still do not plan to have a baby, you should not stick pictures of children on the map. In this case, this sector will be responsible for your creative growth. Think, if you have any creative projects that you would like to implement and find the corresponding images.

In this sector, you can picture all your favourite hobbies and favourite activities and

time for these pleasant activities will come naturally in the near future.

Wisdom and Knowledge Sector

This sector supports the sphere of training. If you wish to enter a prestigious university, then be courageous enough to put the image of the university and the program you would like to study. If you are already studying, you can place images symbolising your learning progress or brilliant graduation from this university. Affirmations will strengthen the work of this sector.

Irina Ahnland

Here you can put all the courses and seminars that you want to attend.

Career, Life Mission and Individuality sector

I suggest that you think very carefully about this aspect of life - career, business (if you want to be self-employed), success and life purpose. You need to see yourself on the next level of your professional activity or business. If you want to change your job, think what your dream job looks like. Where you want to work? What you want to do? What income you would like to get? Would you like to work in a team? Please, write down your answers and think what images to choose for the photo collage in this sector. This could be an image of an office, a building, where you want to work. Place the picture where you look the most serious person at a very prestigious position and you can get down to work (just kidding). Write down affirmations below the image stating your new position, salary, a company where you want to work and your other personal wishes.

If you want to start your dream business or expand the one you already have, you should place relevant images that are associated with successful activities of your business. Your affirmations will manifest your success and desired income.

Right bottom sector symbolises **Travel and Helpful people**. Here you can place pictures of the places you want to visit: Mykonos, Beijing, Tokyo, Majorca, Miami or Antalya. Find the brightest and the most colourful images for this sector and do not even think that you cannot afford your dream vacation. The Treasure Map will perfectly take care of your desire and you will be delighted in the nearest future.

This sector also symbolises helpful people and mentors. Here you can place pictures of your friends or your mentors, who could help and support you.

Now it's time to create your first Treasure Map!

You can easily find pictures and images to your liking on the Internet, old magazines, advertising booklets and theme postcards. Then take your drawing paper and make a square divided into nine parts. The proper size of the Bagua map according to Feng Shui is 68x68 cm, that is each square should have the size 22,66 x22, 66 cm.

Then you either paint the squares in the appropriate colours or stick coloured paper onto them, after this display your pictures and images, starting from the central sector.

When the card is ready, attach it to the wall within your viewing point. You'd better not show the Map to your guests and friends. You should not make it public at this stage because some friends are sceptical and may discourage you. You can take it off and hang back when they leave. It's your biggest dream - your treasure!

Please look at your Treasure Map every day. Imagine that everything you want to have already exists now, in your reality. You have lost weight, feel great, you have even changed your image and style, you have a favourite job, you have improved your accommodation, you have bought a new car, etc.

Imagine that you are already living this life of your dreams and feel in every cell of your body that it has happened. Just because it will be real soon!

One more thing, a Treasure Map is created for a calendar year. If during this year, your dreams come true one after the other, take the old pictures away and stick up the new ones. You can also create a new Treasure Map and remember to appreciate it for its wonderful work of making your cherished dreams and desires come true.

Chapter 12. The letter from the future.

In ancient times, people created time-capsules, these messages were designed to convey historical information for the next generation. Letters were placed in a container with important marks about the time they can be opened and then they were put in a safe place. These capsules were found to contain such items like personal notes, photographs, letters which turned out to be very useful for historians and scholars at that time.

Therefore, it is time for us to write a letter to the future. Who? Yourself!

Yes, it's very unusual task, but it is very effective. Please take it seriously.

The letter will not be from the present day but from the future. Imagine yourself in the next few years. You are in a great shape, energetic, happy and you are enjoying a new life. Your life is filled with bright colours and new challenges that you confront with passion in order to experience this. You can cope with everything and everything is possible for you. Having achieved one goal, you reached the second and the third goal and proved the old truth to be right that "anything is possible if only you desire it very much".

You can choose any form of the letter. Imagine yourself to be perfect and the most attractive in the future, and address yourself at the present moment in order to help you sincerely. Use your imagination and dream a little. At first, you can enjoy the "company" of your future self, chat about life like friends, and when you are ready, start writing the letter.

Describe how your life has changed since you have reached your desired weight by following the Happy Weight Loss program. What is your current job or a new business that you have been dreaming of? Have you got a family, children or new friends? You may also have a new grand purchase, for example, a beautiful house or a new car. How do you feel about your dreams, goals, and challenges? What is now particularly important to you? What else would you like to achieve? How do you spend your free time? What gives you inspiration? Maybe there is something else that Your Future wants to tell you by all means.

If you have fear and anxiety in the present, you can describe how you solved these problems in the future. Ask Your future for advice or ask everything you want to know. Thank him or her for help and support. Remember to write the date, place and sign your letter. Seal the letter in a beautiful envelope and indicate the date when it should be read.

You can read my clients' letters with their permission. Their names are Peter, Tina and Hrisi.

Hello Peter,

I have now reached my ideal weight. I have such a feeling of achievement. I can move more easily, I can run, I can even dance. Life is so much easier without all the extra fat I used to carry around.

I feel more confident, I am no longer embarrassed about myself. I can look in the mirror and the embarrassed fat person is no longer looking at me. I see a slim, strong and healthy man who wants to enjoy his life and go for the dreams. I wish I did it sooner!

I have a lovely new house, three bedrooms. Now I am married to a lovely, kind, faithful woman, we are getting on very well and I love her very much. Every day is wonderful. I love my two new-born children and I love to spend time with my elder daughter Sarah.

At present, I work as a system demonstrator and I love my new job although it involves some travelling, besides, I get a good salary.

I think this is all because of these changes I made some years ago.

May, 2018.

Hello dear Tina,

I was so glad to see you and a piece of my past life, that is your real time where you are now. Please, just do not get frightened next time, because I was also confused and I did not know how to behave myself and what language to speak to you. Well, you've always had a sense of humour and after my booty bounce, you were no longer speechless.

First, you stared at me as if I was an alien and then started to check if my hair, nails and eyelashes were real. Fortunately, you forgot to check my breast. My dear, everything is natural as well as my eyelashes. The secret is my Japanese mascara, the last innovation. Though, it takes more time to remove this beauty, but now you can afford such a luxury. You enjoy yourself, as never before, you are occupied with your favourite business, by the way, it brings a fabulous income ...

It all started with the book that you bought in the bookshop. It was an amazing book, and your transformation was even more amazing. Your every week started with some new crazy idea that could bring you joy. You even wrote a letter to Dalai Lama, and three days later, you already felt his blessings (British post office, of course, does not work so quickly). You lost weight quickly too. You just did not have time to do food shopping like normal people do every Saturday. Luckily, there is a greengrocer next to your house, you just ran out and bought fruits and vegetables when you noticed that your fridge was miserable and empty.

Most of all, I was amused, as you wrote love letters to yourself and ordered the flowers to your address with the most ridiculous names and intriguing messages.

Then the fun began, you got a lot of interesting projects at work; your commission was almost unreal and you decided to start your own business. After going to a restaurant with a friend and celebrating this event with expensive French champagne, you have sketched out a business plan and discussed it in details. Since then you are getting on very well, you're not working for your business, it's your business that works for you, and you just enjoy your life. Now you have enough time to spend more time with your happy family, wonderful friends and interesting activities.

Why am I not looking so great?

Be of good cheer! Well done! You will be there! I love you.

Your Tina, 2018.

Dear Hrisi,

I am you, just three years older and maybe a little bit wiser. There are so many things I wish to say to you and yet I will not as you need to learn them by living them. I will tell you the most important things though!!!

The Hrisi from your future loves you, you are the same person you have always been but without fear anymore. Soon after reading this letter from me, you will stop being afraid. You are no longer afraid of your past (it cannot hurt you!!!). You are no longer afraid of being slim – remember that girl of 18 with long beautiful legs and tiny waist – she was afraid of nothing, she was sexy and she knew it!!! You are still the same personality and will still be in the nearest future.

I remember as soon as I read this letter from the future, I started doing more of what I always enjoyed – walking, cycling, exercising. You are now free to eat the food that truly nourishes your body. Remember you love peaches more than chocolate! Your future is not afraid to be slim, on the contrary, you love your hot body J ! This is the time now to embrace what you always had, you will be there in less than 3 months, believe me!!!

I, Hrisi you are not so distant from your future where you feel love again in your life. All that pain and disappointment is gone, only the good memories remain. Three years from now, you are getting ready for another wedding, this time with a man who truly loves you and cherishes you. You share your newly found passion for horse riding with him and both of you have just moved in the Georgian house you've always wanted. You know that your new You – it was easier than you thought it would be. Love yourself because you are born to make someone really happy and you cannot fully give love if you don't love yourself completely.

You have always dared to get what you wanted, remember how we said we can only get as far as we can dream of getting. Don't stop dreaming, for you shall have it all!!! Have you forgotten there is magic in you when you call for the Universe answers? Have you forgotten who has been watching over you and why do you ever doubt it? Do not listen to other people's right and wrong, you know in your heart what your truth is! I have embraced that divine spark that is in our blood and I am more blessed than ever. Be brave my sister, for you are ever protected! Be brave and embrace that special part of you!

You have stopped regretting what is not to come and what is gone and lost. You have stopped comparing yourself with others and started appreciating yourself and everything about you. If we have lived in different times, you and I would be great generals or fierce queens, do not ever forget it!

Me, the you from the future is wealthy. The business that you are about to start is a happy one but also very profitable. Gali is running it for you as you wanted and you get a healthy cut from it. Your job at Oracle is going very well, I did what your manager told you to do and now I am closing $10 million plus deals. Think big! In the next three years, work will be hard but rewarding and you will achieve financial security. You know it has already begun.

Lastly, I want to tell you that our family is well, mum and dad spend a lot of time with you and the girls are healthy. They are now keenly looking forward to their grandchildren both your and Ve's J.

Before I go my sister remember to look after yourself, eat well and move more, let your fear go off and trust in the Universe to keep you well, for you are loved and protected.

Forever yours,

Hrisi from the future.

Let us wish good luck to Peter, Tina and Hrisi and start writing your letter!

Part IV. Brighten up your life.

Chapter 13. First results – let's have fun.

Today is a special day for you. Today you celebrate your first victory - your first success after 12 weeks. I sincerely believe that you have achieved the desired result, your first goal that you set for yourself at the beginning of the program. So let's celebrate the occasion.

Arrange a party for yourself! Share the fun with others. Celebrate your achievement and then your strengthened confidence will lead you to new heights and even greater success. It is only you who did it all by yourself!

The essence of the celebration is to make this event not only significant, but also memorable. If you celebrate this first success of losing weight in a remarkable way, you will be eager to repeat it again and again, which means that at a subconscious level, you will strive for maximum result and you'll work hard to achieve it.

The word "celebrate" I do not mean tableful with alcoholic beverages, that usually leads to a hangover and the return of the stubborn pounds, we had said goodbye to. This event leaves nothing behind but a headache and a bad mood. The joy of success is intoxicating by itself, so simply celebrate the event with something extraordinary and unusual and express gratitude to yourself.

Your task is to consolidate your positive emotions, feelings of pride and love for yourself and make this day special. This will give you the energy and motivation to become the owner of the beautiful and slender body that you dream about. Find a positive way to mark your new shape.

Here are several ideas you may like to explore:

1. Buy yourself beautiful and expensive clothes, which you've been dreaming of for a long time. Do not economise this time, you deserve to give yourself a gift. Let this thing be a symbol of your achievements and improved shape. Now every time you put these clothes on, remember how well you have done!

2. Share your success with your loved ones and friends; let them express their pride for you. Their kind words of support will further consolidate your subconscious feeling that you can do everything, and to lose weight is the easiest thing for you.

3. Go to a theatre or cinema. Select a funny and inspirational film or a performance and enjoy it, do not forget that you devote the evening to yourself.

4. Invite your friend or your beloved to a restaurant and order your favourite food, just to please yourself, so do not overeat. Do not nickel-and-dime - spend an evening in a big way, with candlelight and live music. Order musicians to play your favourite song, and do not hesitate to ask the waiter for decorated dessert for a special festive occasion. This is your night, so enjoy it entirely.

5. You can just sit back and relax, especially if it has recently been difficult for you to carve out time for yourself.

6. Write about your success on Internet forums or social networks. Then be ready to receive the congratulations and you will notice how your mood improves. People are likely to

respond to the positive messages about the success and they are eager to congratulate you by sending pictures and kind words.

7. Visit an expensive hairdresser and have a chic haircut made. Make your new look even more irresistible. This will lift your spirits, besides, a new haircut will please you for a long time. Just do not forget to persuade the staff in the salon that you usually visit only very expensive hair salons and you are an extremely important and busy person. I wish that you have lots of fun in this role.

If you wish, you may arrange any other thing that gives you pleasure. The main thing is that this option is acceptable and a rare and special occasion for you to some extent.

The next day, write down your feelings, impressions and observations in your Happy Weight Loss dairy. I wish you to achieve even more successful result after the next 12 weeks. Do not be lazy to implement all the recommendations of the book - a healthy and proper diet, work on your eating habits and doing your favourite exercises. It is also important to continue working on visualisation and affirmations, treasure map, remember to keep your diary every day. Besides, the most important thing is to fill your every day with joy and treat yourself with care and love.

Chapter 14. Bring joy into your life.

Nowadays, food is considered to be not only as a source of energy required for our body but it is rather a source of gastronomic delight. Many of us eat not because we are hungry, but because we want to treat ourselves to something delicious.

In the weight loss process when people change their diet and refuse to eat their familiar and favourite foods, this might bring the feeling of dissatisfaction and psychological discomfort. In order to avoid this feeling and make weight loss easy and harmonious fill every day with positive emotions and joyous moments.

Learn to enjoy every moment and simple things: "What a sunny day!", "What a cute baby!", "What beautiful flowers!", etc. Notice everything that seems unusual and beautiful and let it bring you joy! The more joyful moments you find during the day, the more fulfilled it will be, and therefore your life will be more beautiful and more interesting. Remember, we live not only to work every day, but we also live to be happy.

It is important to learn to look at everything in a positive way and try to find something positive in every event. Try to learn how to think in a positive way or think about something pleasant to keep your mind occupied. Smile more often to yourself and to the people around you. Even if you are not used to smiling a lot, force yourself to smile at different occasions. Soon it will become your habit and you will notice how the world is changing around you.

Start your day with a smile and whenever you wake up, just think about pleasant upcoming events. Make the following exercise your tradition each morning. Look at your reflection in the bathroom mirror, where you are not disturbed and express all the love and affection to yourself by asking, "What can I do for such a gorgeous woman or charismatic man today?" Smile and wait a couple of minutes. You will be pleasantly surprised about the answer from your "inner self." So present yourself this gift and your day will be really special.

Every day is important in our human life, so try to fill it with beauty and meaning. Think about each day as a work of art that you are going to create. You have to live and enjoy your life right now and here. Don't think that it's only if you lose weight that you will be happy. Learn to appreciate what you have already got and what surrounded you. Celebrate your every day because day after day, you become healthier and slimmer. This is already a small victory and a reason for joy! The more happy moments you will find in your life, the richer and more graceful your life will be.

A hobby or your favourite activity also can bring you a lot of pleasant emotions and help to bring bright colours in your everyday life. When you are doing things you love, you immerge in a pleasant state of mind, time flies and your soul is singing.

If you have not chosen a hobby yet, but you are interested in this question, I recommend that you listen to yourself. Ponder and recollect the things that you are fond of or what you enjoy doing. Make a list of everything that comes into your head. Then think carefully over each individual item. Use your fantasy to think how you can turn your ideas into reality and proceed to action courageously.

Maybe you had a hobby or something you were particularly interested in as a child. Everyone has a dream to do something or become someone in childhood. When we were little, our mind was not fogged by many problems or rational thinking and our intuition told us about our inner potential. There are few people who are able to make their childhood dreams come true afterall because our life is unpredictable. Our dreams are our hidden talents and creative abilities! Write down everything you remember. If you dreamt of becoming a ballet dancer or a musician, it may be late for you now to make your dream come true, but dancing or playing your favourite musical instrument could be a great hobby which can bring you a lot of inspiration and positive emotions.

For example, analysing childhood dreams helped my client a lot in a similar situation. As a child, she wanted to dance, not just to dance beautifully, but she wanted to be a professional ballet dancer and perform on the big stage, but her dream could not come true due to many circumstances. At present, she is a successful lawyer, she has got a harmonious family with two lovely children. She was 15 kilos overweight and she was very worried about this. All her attempts to lose weight ended in failure. After compiling a personal programme, I advised her to try belly dancing as a new hobby. She was sceptical about this advice at first, but she did not argue with me. Belly dancing is suitable for women of all ages and body types. Two months later, I simply could not recognise her! She lost weight and at the same time she became so attractive and feminine and her eyes just shone with happiness. She became less tired at work and she did not feel backache as she used to do. She also confessed to me that her personal relationship with her husband became passionate, he devoted more time to her and forgot about his friends for meeting up over beer.

Do your best to make your childhood dreams come true and then you will feel happier, more energetic and younger. You can also watch the people around you and note everything that you admire or you like. Make a list of things that fascinate you and choose an interesting activity for yourself.

An exciting hobby will transform your life and it may bring added income as well.

Chapter 15. The miracle of loving yourself.

Do you love yourself? Do you care about yourself? If not, then start surrounding yourself with love and care. It will affect not only your success with a slim figure, but success in all spheres of your life. After all, if you do not love yourself, you are not in harmony with yourself, and thus with the whole world.

Fall in love with yourself and everything around you will change, ranging from your appearance and health to professional and financial successes.

Let's discuss what the love for oneself is, whether it is necessary at all, and how to develop it as a personal quality.

Many people believe that the love for oneself is self-centeredness, arrogance or vanity. But it is far from that. Love for oneself is primarily unconditional self-acceptance. Love for oneself is the most precious gift you can ever give yourself. If you love and appreciate yourself, then you are harmonious and happy. You give the world only the good and creative impact. You shine with joy and love all around you. It is only by learning to understand and accept yourself that we will learn to understand, accept and love others.

Just imagine how a person can be kind and compassionate to other people, if he is not good and tolerant with himself. Can he give the other person love and tenderness if he does not know how to express love and attention to himself? After all, you cannot give anything that does not exist ... Think about it. It is no accident there is a sentence in the Bible: "You shall love your neighbour as yourself" (Lev.19: 18). Mind the key phrase "as yourself ".

Just accept yourself for who you are and forget about all your shortcomings, especially regarding your shape. It is only temporary. I truly believe that you have already put all the principles of the Happy Weight Loss program in action and you have seen your first results. Please be a little patient to approach your ideal weight. It will not be difficult, believe me.

Now let's discuss in detail how you can express love to yourself.

Love life!

If you start loving life with all your heart, with every single cell in you, with every breath, tender-care, trustingly, romantically and passionately then life will love you with the same force. Consequently, the most amazing wonders will happen if the whole world is conspiring to surprise and delight you every moment.

Just try to fall in love with life, and then it will be the most mutual, happy and exciting love story that can be experienced!

The main thing is to be thankful, always thank your life, for all its treasures that it presents you so generously.

Write a love letter to yourself!

This is a very interesting and exciting effective technique - a love letter. To who, take a guess! To yourself of course. Have you ever written love letters to yourself? If not, then do write and send it today, of course, to your own address. A few days later write another letter and send it back. Write letters to yourself every week and more often if you can. When did you receive love letters by mail the last time? It's hard to say, now you'll regularly receive them from the dearest and the most important person from yourself. The letters do not need to be long and meaningful; they may consist only of a few sentences. The main thing is that you are able to express the most beautiful feelings and gratitude for yourself. How often we criticize ourselves and how seldom we thank ... and now you have this opportunity to do it in the most romantic and unusual way. Please try and you will be pleasantly surprised!

Do not compare yourself with others

Comparing yourself with others is one of the most widespread daily habits. If you think that you are imperfect in some way, just forget about it at once. Nobody is perfect, either externally or internally. You are a unique, special and amazing person and there is nobody like you. This is your value and if you came into this world, then the world really needs you!

Compare yourself only with yourself both in the past and in the present. Notice all the good things that you have done today, even if it is just a couple of things. Think of the things that you have achieved during the last 6-12 months, what traits you were able to change in yourself, consider your progress towards your goal or a dream. Be sure to congratulate yourself, write about your progress in the diary and follow the dynamics of the process.

Learn to be yourself and reach your goals, even if your idea of happiness or success does not coincide with the opinion of others - colleagues, friends or public opinion. Please do not judge them for it. You are unique, so your perception of the world is unique and therefore all your dreams are unique too! Live only for your dreams and just be yourself!

Give yourself a compliment every time you pass the mirror!

Every time you pass a mirror, compliment yourself - out loud or silently. Notice every positive, even the smallest detail.

For example, how fresh you look today or how cool you look in your new clothes. Do not pass a mirror without looking at yourself with love and saying to yourself something good even in thought. If at first you find it difficult to do this exercise and it is hard for you to praise your reflection, do not force yourself. Just start looking in the mirrors more often, those mirrors that you avoided before. In a couple of weeks, you will begin to learn how to compliment yourself for the first time after a long time. I bet in the next couple of weeks, it will be hard to draw you away from looking in the mirror, admiring your own reflection.

And if all of a sudden you meet a passer-by practicing the same, do not hesitate to give her / him a compliment. Now you know how to do it!

Pamper yourself

Ask yourself more often, what your soul wants right now. It will tell you something by all means, so go ahead and treat yourself right now without putting it off till tomorrow. The more you give yourself a treat during the day, the better.

Every day do something that you enjoy, that makes you happy and makes your heart glad. This will be a great opportunity to express your love for yourself.

The most important thing is to allow yourself to rest when you are tired. Do something pleasant that will help you relax: take a warm bath, watch your favourite movie or a TV show, read a book, listen to music or just lie down on the sofa! You deserve it!

Communicate with positive people and avoid negative events

Communication with positive people lifts up our spirits, gives us enthusiasm and a desire to take an action or create something enjoyable. A positive person is overwhelming with energy, so after talking with a positive person, we even feel physically better but you can experience an opposite situation if you meet a negative person who can might law your spirit or even lead to an emotional breakdown.

The best solution here is to limit your communication with negative people and increase your level of communication with positive people.

Have your picture taken more often!

Life is so splendid and amazing but unfortunately it flies. Get your pictures taken and capture the most joyful and exciting moments in your life. You will once again relive the events depicted in them and feel great pleasure watching them with your loved ones or just alone. Take your camera with you and take pictures of yourself, your family and friends. Catch the exciting moments that happen to you and all the beautiful things surrounding you and your life will become more joyful, wonderful and rich.

Do not forget about your appearance

Take care of your appearance and always try to look attractive and neat. Always have light make-up, good perfumes and colognes. Visit hairdressing and beauty salons more often. From time to time buy yourself something nice and useful at the same time to express yourself: a new handbag, shoes, scarves and other accessories.

Chapter 16. Fitness for pleasure, Fitness for fun.

"Movement is life," the ancient Greeks said. Physical activity is essential for our body to function properly and stay healthy. Lack of exercise is as dangerous to a human as the lack of oxygen, water and nutrients. Physical activity helps us to be slim, healthy and beautiful.

Unfortunately, not many of us can boast of regular sports activities, and the reason for it is not lack of free time or willpower but the wrong attitude about it. Sport causes negative emotions and anger for some people. It is because you need to make an effort first go to the gym and then you have to sacrifice your precious time. There may be a red carpet on the floor but unluckily you will not see petals of fresh roses. A real torture is waiting for already exhausted people, i.e. the work with muscles which can hardly be visible. More importantly, you are expected to have a facial expression of a fitness fanatic who is attending the gym for the second time today. As a result, such activity does not become a regular and integral part of our life because it does not bring pleasure and excitement.

We need positive emotions, brightness, rhythm and drive. We need a sport for fun and for joy. I bet that you can easily recall several such kinds of sport. It can be swimming, cycling, dancing or dance aerobics, skating or rollerblading, soccer and event walking in the park will bring you fun and be good for your health.

If you have chosen a kind of sport of your liking, I suggest you take the next step and it is the most interesting part, you will learn how to make exercises an enjoyable habit. I'd like to share an important discovery with you, which I have made in my research. Just imagine, people are not born to be fitness fanatics, they become one during their life! Are you interested in secrets of their regular work and training? So here they are:

1. No goals first, only pleasant pastime.

At the moment, it is not worth setting a goal to have 60 cm waist, splendid hips or super muscled body. *(It is worth setting up goals but not at his point, when you just started to do sport.)* All you need is to take physical exercise as a fun activity. Just make your exercises joyful and interesting.

Be creative. If you're going to start with swimming, invite a friend and promise her that you'll swim just to make your swimsuit wet and the rest of the time you'll spend in the sauna, rubbing yourselves with different scrubs or drink tea in the relaxation room sharing the latest gossip.

2. Begin with short but regular sessions.

The sessions should last only 7 - 10 minutes, but three times a week. It is very easy and it takes little effort. Turn on a few of your favourite songs and do a few press-ups, push-ups and squats. If you have got an aerobic step bench, do 50-70 step-ups, it is a great way to shape your legs and hips. Do hula hooping or just dance to the music.

The first session should not be longer than 7-10 mins and let the movements be joyful! Then a good mood and some excitement is guaranteed all day long or for the rest of the evening!

3 Put on beautiful sportswear during fitness sessions.

Choose only bright and beautiful sportswear for your fitness classes. You must like your look and feel happier. If your cute tummy is baggy somewhere, never mind, it is only temporary, believe me. You can fool around in front of a mirror before your fitness session, for example, shake your booty or show your biceps. Always wear only a beautiful sports outfit even if you exercise at home. Because every day is special and now you decide to give a gift to your body. I promise that your husband will immediately finish his important work and admire how beautiful, attractive and sporty you look while doing your exercises. If you have children, they will be happy to join you and have fun repeating the exercises with you.

4. Avoid monotony.

Make your sessions varied and interesting. Regularly change your exercise or training program and avoid boring workouts. If you exercise at home, choose energetic dance music for your sessions.

5. Motivate and reward yourself.

Let a new good habit be your main goal and as well as positive emotions which are usually formed after sporting activity. Just motivate yourself that it's time to move your beloved body, lift up your spirit and once again, prove the world that you are a Supergirl or Superman. After the training think very hard about how you can spoil yourself with something or make something pleasant for yourself. It is a real deed again, so why not?

6. Keep notes.

You can write down just a couple of words in your Happy Weight Loss dairy, but it will be a wonderful way to see your progress and motivate you into further fitness activity. Just briefly note down in your diary the activity that you did and its duration (e.g. 'running 20 minutes' or 'dance aerobics' 1 hour).

The last but the most important tip.

Smile at your reflection in the mirror and send yourself a kiss!

Do fitness for pleasure and joy and you will not wait long to see the result! Good luck to you!

Chapter 17. Brand New You, Big celebration.

Today, you have a special day - the day when your dream has finally come true. You've become the owner of your dream shape. You did it, didn't you! It is worthwhile celebrating this event, so let's make this day a fireworks of unforgettable impressions.

Use your imagination and make an original screenplay. This event may take place in your favourite restaurant or a karaoke bar, a club, a house or in any original place. Do not forget to send beautiful and intriguing invitation cards to your friends. I can give you a few tips, If you want to have a lot of fun.

Create your new personalised photo calendars with your new look and send them to your friends, and soon your phone will be ringing constantly. Hope your friend will not think that that your hamster died and your suffering over its death so much that you lost 20 kilos. Do not hesitate to tell people about your success.

You can also make money with your pictures as a joke and share it with your friends, relatives, colleagues and all the people who need it. Remember to send me a couple of notes, I'll try to arrange charity with it.

Ask musicians to write a song about you, praising how cool you are now and upload this song on your phone instead of threatening alarm clock signals. I guarantee you will wake up with a smile. You can also present your friends with your new hit to set it up as a ringtone with your name. Your friends will know when you are calling them. The secret is that they will call you for no reason, and it's not because you became so much slimmer, but the reason is that you now live a happy life and you are in love with your life or the life is desperately in love with you, so that it keeps pleasing you with delightful surprises and gifts.

Okay, let's go back to the organization of the celebration.

It is worthwhile decorating the place for your party celebration with fresh flowers, balloons, ribbons – all of your favourite and festive colours. It's the most important to remember to show your pictures before and after weight loss. Do not feel shy about your previous pictures, treat your past self with humour and surprise the guests with your stunning results.

Equip yourself with a camera. In fact, video and good pictures will pleasantly remind you of one of the most wonderful days in your life.

You can also have fun in a completely different way by arranging a theme party so that you will have unusual, bright and awesome times.

The most popular and easy ways to set up themes party are:

Hawaiian or beach party. Ladies wear bathing suits, young men wear Hawaiian shorts. Everything is bright, beachfront, joyful. Particular attention should be paid to the music (Hawaiian catchy rhythms) and food (summer menu includes lots of fruit, juices and cocktails). Interior accessories - all kinds of straw, wicker items, beach umbrellas, deck chairs, big pictures of the sea and sand hanging on the walls.

Movie Party. Each guest chooses his favourite movie character and imitates his or her image in dress, manners. Use posters with celebrities to decorate the room; transform the room into a dressing room, select a place for the stage.

Irina Ahnland

The same thing can be done with literary characters and images.

National Party. Select a country and represent exactly its culture and traditions, including the cuisine and the costumes, music and national features. As another option, you can organise a multinational party where everyone represents a certain country, it is desirable to "act out" your role: you can learn a few words in the language of that country, funny cultural traditions and bring ready-made traditional food and cocktails.

Perhaps one of the most unusual and amusing ways of celebrating your weight loss may be a holiday with a balloon flight. Nowadays, it is quite affordable to arrange yourself such a flight. You can find special companies organising such events in almost every city.

To see the world from this height is an amazing and exciting experience. Order a tethered hot air balloon to host a big company so that all your guests will feel comfortable on the same balloon. The balloon will resemble a tourist attraction: the sky, the altitude of the bird's flight, flowers, champagne and congratulations on your new shape - what could be better than that! You can also arrange the competition in climbing up to the sky if you order a few balloons.

Invite your closest friends, whom you want to share your success with and thoroughly prepare to conquer the sky. Get all the information from the organising company, discuss all their services. Specify all the details and insurance for all participants. Find out the weather forecast and make sure it is not going to rain or low clouds and strong wind will not interfere with your plans for that day. If this is OK, then you will have an unforgettable day!

By celebrating your achievements, you draw a connection between the success and the upcoming reward in your subconscious mind. Subsequently, you will unconsciously strive for new achievements to get the reward. Your subconscious mind will help you to overcome laziness and will motivate you to conquer new heights.

Celebrating your success, both big or small achievements and you will discover more and more reasons for the party!

Conclusion

It is time for the anxious moment of finishing the book. I hope very much that during the weight loss process, you enjoyed yourself a lot and entertained your friends with happy events celebrating the lost kilos and new habits. Someone may have followed your example and has started an amazing journey of transformation. No doubt, fruit and vegetables are decorating your kitchen, bright and beautiful clothes are gorgeously hanging in your wardrobe. You have almost stopped watching TV and spend more time outdoors or in the company of your family and friends. Your diary constantly reminds you not only about important things, but also about leisure time, funny tricks and your favourite sports activities. On the way to work you no longer read boring news and threatening forecasts, but quietly close your eyes and daydream about something amazing, visualising it in your imagination. You regularly get tender love letters from yourself and your friends have much fun sending you letters 'from your future and from your past'.

I am really very glad for you. Be happy today, tomorrow and always! Love yourself and love life! Enjoy small things and notice the beauty in simplicity and then every day will be a masterpiece for you. Do not miss it ... because there is only one Today.

Create a new dream, achieve it and let it inspire you. Conquer new peaks, appreciate every moment, give love and joy to your loved ones because our life is only one and it flies so fast.

Your Irina Anland,

With love.

P.S. Please send me your happy stories about your weight loss experience and tell me how your life has changed. Remember to write about the celebration of your new shape. Your examples will inspire others and help them to strive to achieve their goal and resist the temptations.

Contact Irina Ahnland via email: ahnlandi@yahoo.co.uk or visit the website: www.weightlossirina.com

Printed in Great Britain
by Amazon

78260091R00068